Praise for *The Positive Intent Mindset*

"This book will change how you interpret others—and transform how you lead. In a world quick to assume the worst, this book offers the powerful—and refreshingly doable—alternative of choosing curiosity, assuming good intent, and leading with empathy."
DORIE CLARK, executive education faculty at Columbia Business School, *Wall Street Journal* bestselling author of *The Long Game*

"*The Positive Intent Mindset* shows leaders how to build trust and transform relationships by learning to assume the best in others without compromising accountability. Especially by taking a pause to use our more rational brains to increase our empathy for others and find better solutions. Through thorough research, compelling stories, and practical insights, Amer Kaissi shows how choosing a mindset of realistic optimism, empathy, and humility can help build stronger teams and lead to impactful results."
MARIA ROSS, TEDx speaker, author of *The Empathy Edge* and *The Empathy Dilemma*

"*The Positive Intent Mindset* shows that assuming good intent is far from naïveté—it's a courageous, data-driven choice with remarkable benefits. It's not just the right thing to do but the smart thing to do."
DR. STEPHEN TRZECIAK AND DR. ANTHONY MAZZARELLI, bestselling authors of *Compassionomics* and *The Wonder Drug*

The Positive Intent Mindset

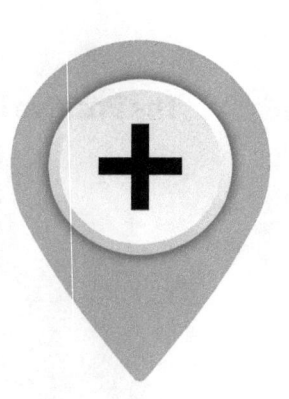

The Positive Intent Mindset

Exceptional Leadership Through Trust and Accountability

AMER KAISSI

PAGE TWO

Copyright © 2025 by Amer Kaissi

All rights reserved. No part of this book may be reproduced, stored in a retrieval system or transmitted, in any form or by any means, without the prior written consent of the publisher, except in the case of brief quotations, embodied in reviews and articles.

Some names and identifying details have been changed to protect the privacy of individuals.

Cataloguing in publication information is available from Library and Archives Canada.
ISBN 978-1-77458-615-0 (paperback)
ISBN 978-1-77458-616-7 (ebook)

Page Two
pagetwo.com

Page Two™ is a trademark owned by Page Two Strategies Inc., and is used under license by authorized licensees

Cover, interior design, and illustrations by Cameron McKague

amerkaissi.com

Dedicated to my wife, kids, parents, and brother
And to my amazing students at Trinity University

Contents

Foreword *1*

1. **Our Choice** *5*
2. **Why All the Negativity?** *17*
3. **How Accountable Positivity Works** *29*
4. **The Limits** *43*
5. **Making It Work** *53*
6. **Realistic Optimism** *65*
7. **Empathy** *79*
8. **Humility** *93*
9. **Reality Testing** *105*
10. **Forgiveness** *119*
11. **The Positive Intent Organization** *131*

Acknowledgments *135*

Notes *137*

Foreword

IN OUR research as physician-scientists and healthcare leaders, we have always been drawn to examining the science of concepts typically relegated to the moral, ethical, or emotional domains. W. Edwards Deming once said, "Without data, you're just another person with an opinion." This principle has guided our work, as we believe in the primacy of empirically grounded approaches not just in medicine but in how we live our lives.

In our book *Compassionomics*, we asked if compassion really matters in healthcare, reviewing over 500 abstracts and peer-reviewed journals and concluding that compassion impacts outcomes in meaningful and *measurable* ways. In *Wonder Drug*, we extended this research to show how serving others can be life-changing therapy for everyone, everywhere—not just in healthcare settings. The scientific evidence was clear: Being others-focused is not only the right thing to do but also the *smart* thing to do.

When we encountered Dr. Amer Kaissi's work on assuming good intent, we recognized a natural extension of this evidence-based approach to human relationships. We felt like it builds on the strength of his work in *Humbitious*. What initially seems like a simple concept—choosing to believe others are acting with positive intentions—is revealed through rigorous examination to be a powerful tool with profound implications for individuals, teams, and organizations. Amer's *The Positive Intent Mindset* shows that assuming good intent is far from naïveté—it's a courageous, data-driven choice with remarkable benefits. Again, it's not just the right thing to do but the smart thing to do.

For years, we've observed how assumptions about intent shape interactions in healthcare environments. When a new leader joins our 137-year-old health system and identifies a process that seems inefficient or problematic, we share the perspective that there are typically three possibilities: Someone designed it that way due to incompetence, someone created it with malicious intent, or—most likely—someone designed it with the best intentions based on the resources and circumstances of that time. We encourage leaders to begin by assuming the third explanation and require compelling evidence before considering the first two. This approach has transformed countless potentially adversarial interactions into collaborative problem-solving opportunities. Amer's book provides a structure to this approach and explains the science behind these observations.

What makes his work so valuable is that it moves beyond platitudes about positivity. This is not fluffy, pie-in-the-sky thinking. Instead, it provides evidence-based tools for assuming good intent while maintaining accountability. The research Amer presents demonstrates that assuming good intent is beneficial not only for the subject of the assumption but also for the person making it—a fascinating parallel to our findings about serving others.

As we transition from the knowledge economy to an era where artificial intelligence will make information increasingly accessible, the premium skill will not be subject matter expertise but rather the ability to connect meaningfully with other people. Assuming good intent is a cornerstone of this ability.

The research presented in these pages shows that assuming good intent, like compassion and service to others, activates neurological pathways associated with positive emotions and shifts our nervous systems towards states of calm. It buffers against chronic stress, improves team functioning, and creates environments where innovation and problem-solving flourish. Perhaps most importantly, it helps us see beyond surface behaviors to understand the authentic human experiences driving them.

We are in an era where assuming negative intent has become the default in many spheres. Social media algorithms reward outrage, news cycles capitalize on conflict, and political discourse often begins with the assumption that those who disagree with us are not just wrong but malevolent. In this context, Amer's work is not just timely but essential.

As you read this book, we encourage you to approach it as a scientist—examine the evidence, consider its applications to your life and work, and test its principles. But also approach it as a human who recognizes that the quality of our lives is largely determined by the quality of our relationships.

The evidence-based path forward is clear: Assume good intent, hold yourself and others accountable with compassion, and watch as your interactions, teams, and organizations transform. The barrier to entry is small, yet the impact is seismic. That journey begins with what follows in these pages.

Stephen Trzeciak, MD, MPH
Edward D. Viner Endowed Chief of Medicine
Cooper University Health Care
Professor and Chair of Medicine
Cooper Medical School of Rowan University

Anthony Mazzarelli, MD, JD, MBE
Co-President/Chief Executive Officer
Cooper University Health Care
Dean of Clinical Affairs
Cooper Medical School of Rowan University

— 1 —

Our Choice

MY FRIEND Hunter leads a small team. At one point they had a vacancy and were excited to be able to hire an internal candidate, Tina, who was on the team whose offices were right next door. At that time, Hunter and his team were getting ready to launch a big event, and Tina was going to play a major role in it. Hunter talked to her manager and they agreed that Tina would have a four-week transition period to finish her projects with her old team before joining Hunter's.

Now the transition period is over, it's the start of a new week, and Tina is supposed to begin working full-time on Hunter's team. It's Monday morning. Hunter is on his way to the restroom when he passes by the other team's glass-walled conference room and sees Tina sitting there in a meeting with her old team. He is a bit annoyed by it, so an hour later, he calls their manager to ask him what is going on. The manager explains, "Yeah, you're right, I am sorry, I asked Tina to come back one last time because I needed her to wrap up a few things."

"Okay, no problem," says Hunter. "I understand."

Hunter and his team keep busy preparing for the big launch. Now it's the start of the second week, and when Hunter passes by the other team's conference room, he sees Tina in there again, in a meeting with her old team. Hunter starts boiling. He feels so disrespected. He is stressed out about the launch, and it looks like Tina couldn't care less, sitting there and chitchatting with her old friends. Without thinking, Hunter barges into the meeting, confronts Tina, and says, "What are you still doing here? Your transition was over more than two weeks ago, and I need you for the launch!"

Tina and the other manager are both stunned. After Hunter stops shouting, the manager explains: "Hunter, we know about the big launch, and actually Tina is here because she is sharing the details of your launch with our team so we can figure out how to help you." Hunter stands there, embarrassed. He had assumed the worst about Tina's intentions, questioning her commitment to her new team. And yet here she was, working hard and capitalizing on her existing relationships to make his launch succeed. Can his relationship with Tina ever recover? Can she trust him again as her leader?

THROUGH MY OWN EXPERIENCES, which include working with hundreds of leaders over the years, I have come to believe that how we think about other people determines to a large extent how we interact with them and how we feel about ourselves. Obviously, this is not a new idea. Thousands of years ago Epictetus asserted, "It is not things that disturb us, but our interpretation of their significance." Shakespeare famously wrote, "There is nothing either good or bad but thinking makes it so." And John Milton said, "The mind is its own place, and in itself can make a heaven of hell, and a hell of heaven."

I grew up in Beirut, Lebanon, during the Lebanese Civil War. From that experience I learned that when people make negative assumptions about each other's intentions because of politics and religion, horrible things can happen to whole societies. And having worked as an educator and executive coach since moving to the US 25 years ago, I have seen how this pattern of mistrust hurts my students and the leaders I work with, wreaking havoc on their well-being and mental health.

How we think about other people is significantly influenced by the assumptions we make about their intentions. If we assume someone is out to get us, we interpret their words and actions accordingly. And that negatively impacts how we feel about them when we interact with them. If we learn to examine our assumptions and replace negative ones with positive or even neutral ones, we can significantly improve our relationships with others. But most importantly, examining our assumptions can help us feel better and experience inner peace and happiness. This is the basic premise of this book.

For human beings, assuming the worst about others' intentions appears to be hardwired into our brains. It stems from fear and insecurity, and it can actually protect us in life-threatening situations. But most work and personal situations today are not life-threatening. Constantly assuming negative intent is maladaptive; it can ruin our relationships and make us feel constantly miserable.

Another reason we react this way is the wide availability of overwhelmingly negative information. It is not the world itself that is more negative these days; it's that negative news is much more accessible and promoted. Scrolling on our phones, we can read about genocides, murders, scams, and scandals before we have even had our morning coffee. As these bits of news poison our brains daily, it is no surprise we assume that most people are dishonest and have negative intentions.

To overcome this, we need to rewire our brains: Instead of fear, insecurity, and self-protection, we need to learn realistic optimism, empathy, humility, reality testing, and forgiveness. And that mindset change requires intentionality and consistency, which sounds simple but is actually very hard to do in our busy professional lives. Most reasonable people would agree it's better to assume that people's intentions are positive, but very few are able to practice this mindset consistently. That is why I wrote this book: to provide a simple guide to rewiring our brains, improving our relationships at work and elsewhere, rebuilding trust with others, and finding some inner contentment.

ASSUMING POSITIVE INTENTIONS takes a lot of commitment, and for many of us the promise that it will benefit our relationships with other people is not enough.

So, allow me to argue that the most important reason to make this change is not to benefit others. It is for *yourself*.

Donovan, a colleague of mine, told me once about an incident that happened in his first few months at his new job. Donovan is a young African American man. He was put in charge of organizing the educational sessions for his team every two weeks, which included ordering the food. After the first few sessions, some team members asked Donovan if he could get healthier options instead of just chips and cookies. At the next session, Donovan brought only fruits and yogurt. Claudia, another team member (and a white woman), arrived early and when she saw that the healthy options had replaced the regular snacks, she half jokingly said, "No one is going to like this, Donovan. You're going to get lynched!"

Donovan was stunned. He didn't know how to react, so he stayed quiet. Throughout the day he couldn't stop thinking about the word *lynched*, so as soon as he got home that evening, he called his father to share what had happened and ask for advice. His father told him he was well within his rights to go to human resources and report the incident as an act of racism.

But Donovan didn't want to punish Claudia—he wanted to understand her. So instead of reporting her, he sent her an email and requested to meet with her. At the meeting, Donovan asked her if she was aware of the impact the word she used had had on him. Claudia said she wasn't. So, Donovan very patiently explained to her the connotation that the word *lynched* has for an African American man. Claudia apologized and said she didn't mean any harm; she was just making a joke. In that moment, Donovan decided to believe she was ignorant, not racist.

When Donovan shared the incident with me, I asked him why he decided to give Claudia the benefit of the doubt. He told me, "I didn't do it for her. I did it for me. Of course, there is a high chance that she is actually a racist and that she lied about not knowing the impact of that word. But I didn't want to carry that burden with me forever. So, I chose to forgive her." Instead of calling her out, he did what activist and professor Loretta Ross refers to as calling *in*—he held her accountable without making strong accusations that would have made her defensive and prevented the possible learning opportunity. Now, of course, if Claudia repeats this behavior in the future, Donovan will not be as understanding.

I share this not to suggest that we should give every racist and sexist colleague the benefit of the doubt. Of course they should be held accountable for their actions; not every person that belongs to a marginalized group will feel and act like Donovan did, nor should they be expected to. I share this story to show that Donovan realized he had a choice: He could assume negative intentions and feel like a victim, or he could assume positive intentions and seek to understand. He felt much better when he chose the latter. He made the choice for *himself*.

My larger point is this: When another person—whether we know them well or not—acts in a way that annoys, harms, or hurts us, we feel pain. We experience it in every fiber of our being. Pain is inevitable—but *suffering is optional*.

When you're driving to work and a car violently cuts you off, you feel angry and even scared. There is nothing you can do about those initial feelings because they are a natural reaction. However, what you do next is totally under your control: how you interpret the incident, how long you think about it, and how much space you allow it to occupy in your head throughout the day.

If you convince yourself that the other driver is a reckless jerk, you will be tempted to speed up so that you can get close enough to yell at them, or maybe even give them the finger. The other driver may return the favor, which will only increase your anger. Then they may take an exit and disappear, but you will keep thinking about the incident all the way to work: "How can anyone drive like this? Why don't the police do something about these people?" At work, you keep stewing about it. You go to your first meeting still angry, and when you recount to your team what happened, you relive the incident and experience the same intense feelings. Throughout the morning, you are unfocused and distracted. You have enabled all this suffering, and it has ruined your day.

Imagine, on the other hand, that as soon as the other driver cuts you off and you feel the strong reaction, you remind yourself to take a deep breath. You decide to give the other driver the benefit of the doubt—instead of a reckless jerk, could they be a parent racing their child to the nearest hospital? The moment you bring yourself to think of them as a human being and not a monster, your suffering starts to ease. A few moments later, you will yourself to turn on some good music and you continue on your way. You arrive at work relaxed and lead your meeting effectively. You barely think about that incident again for the whole day.

Which day sounds better to you? And which day results in more inner contentment and better well-being?

Now, let's be clear: It is very likely that the other driver was in fact a reckless jerk. Yes, there are plenty of jerks out there who care only about themselves and drive like maniacs even if they don't have an emergency. But why should we worry about that? What is the benefit of unnecessary suffering? Nothing. No one cares if you spend the whole day stewing or forget about it right way. Certainly, the jerk doesn't care—they didn't think about you in the first place, and they will never think about you again. So, what is the point of continuing to think about *them*?

The Buddha talked about a similar concept in his parable of the first arrow and the second arrow. He explained that if you are hit with an arrow, the pain from the impact is real. But if you start feeling bad about being hit, that's a second arrow—and the emotional suffering it causes is up to you. We cannot control the first arrow, whether it is physical or verbal, but we can control the second one, which is non-physical and comes from within. How we deal with the second arrow determines the extent of our suffering. The minute we stop thinking about something in a negative way, that is the start of our inner peace and happiness.

BUT THERE IS ANOTHER piece to this, and it's no less important. Assuming positive intent does *not* mean we should be blithely oblivious to negativity or paper over problems. We need to constantly seek the upper-right corner on the Intent and Accountability Matrix.

Intent and Accountability Matrix

	Assuming Negative Intent	Assuming Positive Intent
High Accountability	Aggressive Toxicity	Accountable Positivity
Low Accountability	Passive Toxicity	Toxic Positivity

Here's how the matrix usually plays out:

- In a team where assuming positive intent is combined with low accountability, a culture of toxic positivity is created. Every conflict, disagreement, and wrong behavior is swept under the rug under the pretext that "we should all get along."

- At the other extreme, in teams whose members assume negative intent while holding each other accountable at very high standards, a culture of aggressive toxicity is created. That culture is characterized by low trust and collaboration, and high anxiety. Conflict based on personal agendas and politics is prevalent, and backstabbing is rampant.

- Meanwhile, in teams that assume negative intent and don't verify it, accountability is ignored and passive toxicity is created. People spread rumors about each other, and apathy prevails.

- The best teams and cultures are those where people assume positive intent *and* hold each other accountable for their words and actions. Accountable positivity results in trust, collaboration, and peace of mind.

Assuming positive intent is not a naïve approach to relationships and life. There are jerks and rotten people out there who intend to hurt others, but all the scientific, historical, social, and psychological evidence suggests that they are a very small minority. We are better off assuming positive intent, even if people will take advantage of us on occasion. Positivity is a much more productive way to live and lead, as long as it is *accountable*—not used to let people off the hook and ignore bad behaviors.

The point is that we have control over how we think about events. We are involved in creating our reality. And shifting to the positive intent mindset not only makes us feel better but also makes us better leaders, because it leads to better interactions with others, more collaboration, and improved outcomes. Indra Nooyi, the highly successful former CEO of PepsiCo, once advised, "Whatever anybody says or does, assume positive intent. You will be amazed at how your whole approach to a person or problem becomes very different. When you assume negative intent, you're angry. If you take away that anger and assume positive intent, you will be amazed."

This book is about how we can make that work... *realistically*.

— 2 —

Why All the Negativity?

Last year, I was giving a leadership workshop in a hotel conference room to a group of healthcare executives. Ten minutes into the presentation, a hotel employee—an older woman—suddenly opens the door, walks across the room, and delivers a cup of coffee to an executive sitting in the front row. I am shocked and irritated, thinking, "Who is this guy? And why is he having coffee delivered to his seat in the middle of my workshop? Can't he bring his own coffee? The coffee station is right outside the door!"

The employee leaves, and I'm trying to go back to my content but am still irritated. This guy is so inconsiderate. He interrupted the flow of the workshop and bothered everyone. I occasionally glare at him as he is happily sipping his coffee.

A while later we take a break, and the executive immediately comes up to me and introduces himself as Tim. He says, "I am so sorry for the disruption. You probably think I am a jerk and ordered the coffee delivered to me, but I swear that's not what happened!" He then tells me he had met Daniela, the woman who brought him the coffee, the previous evening at the event reception. He talked to her and asked her about her family, and she was happy to share. Towards the end of the reception, he noticed she was working all by herself, so he decided to help her clean up. Daniela couldn't believe he was helping her. She told him that no one had ever done that before.

This morning, Tim said, he had woken up a bit late and came down looking for coffee before the workshop started. But the coffee pitcher was empty. Daniela was there and promised she would bring another pitcher soon, but Tim had to go into the conference room because the workshop was about to start. When Daniela came back with the full pitcher and didn't see Tim outside, she took it upon herself to pour him a big cup and deliver it to him to thank him for what he did the previous night.

I stood there stunned. I had assumed the worst about Tim. I thought he was entitled and inconsiderate. But it turns out he is the kindest guy in the world, the type of guy who gets to know the hotel staff and even helps them clean up. I had judged Tim without giving him any benefit of the doubt. (Just to make sure, I later on checked the story separately with Daniela, and she confirmed it word by word. I am not naïve!)

FOR MOST of us, assuming the worst is our default setting. We are wired to judge and not to trust, because that is how we have always protected ourselves from possible dangers. In prehistoric times, when a cave person encountered someone they had never seen before, they assumed the worst about them: This creature will hurt me or kill me. And in that case it was definitely the right approach to stay safe and survive. If they assumed negative intention and protected themselves and the other person indeed turned out to be a threat, they may have saved their own life. If the other person somehow turned out to be friendly, there was no harm done. Likewise, if the cave person was on their way to get water and heard an animal in the bushes, it was in their best interest to assume it was dangerous and change their route. If the animal turned out be a harmless deer, the only disadvantage was walking an extra half hour. Because the world was so dangerous, fear was beneficial most of the time and created some inconveniences only on a few occasions.

Another reason we assume negative intentions is insecurity. We need to maintain not just physical safety but social position—this, too, was important for survival in prehistoric times, and we still feel social gains and losses sharply. Part of the reason I got so irritated by the coffee being delivered inside the conference room is that I felt my authority as a speaker was being threatened. If people were ordering coffee in the middle of my presentation, that meant they didn't respect me, so to protect myself I assumed Tim had negative intent.

These self-protective instincts make most of us focus more on avoiding loss than seeking gain, even in interpersonal relationships. When it comes to our assumptions about the behaviors of others, there are four possible scenarios:

	The other person behaves positively	The other person behaves negatively
I assume positive intentions	Trust is built	I get burned
I assume negative intentions	The relationship is damaged	I protect myself

As you see from the table, trust comes with gains but also makes us vulnerable. So, because we are loss-averse, we default to self-protection—even though, as we have seen, in the great majority of cases the other person will behave positively.

As adaptive evolutionary responses designed to keep us safe, fear and self-protection are appropriate. But constant fear can be unproductive and unhealthy. Despite what we might think, the world is a much safer place today and continues to become safer and safer. In his well-researched book *The Better Angels of Our Nature*, the Canadian-American cognitive psychologist Steven Pinker argues that we are actually living in the most peaceful moment in our species' existence. Since the development of agriculture around 10,000 years ago, murder and violence rates have been going down and have dropped significantly since the Middle Ages in particular. Even in more recent years, data from the Federal Bureau of Investigation and Bureau of Justice Statistics clearly shows a significant decrease in rates of violence and property crime in the US between 1993 and 2022.

And yet many of us get more and more fearful every year. As I mentioned in chapter 1, this fear is directly related to what we consume in social media and on cable news. On any typical morning, if we scroll on our phones or watch any major TV network for 10 minutes, we are likely to hear about a murder that happened overnight in our city, a mass killing in a war across the world, a corporate scandal in a large multinational company, or a financial scam in our own country. But it is not that these negative events are happening more frequently now—it's that modern technology has given us the ability to learn about them in a much more efficient and condensed way.

The problem is that our brains are not designed to deal with all this negativity all at once. The average person living in a small town in the 1600s probably heard about just a handful of murders, scams, and mass killings in their *lifetime*. While the world was much more dangerous, most people only knew about what happened in their own small world, and even that only through word of mouth. Today, the average person hears about numerous murders, scams, and mass killings *every day*, because all the information is available in their palms.

For a long time media companies have exploited the evolutionary fact that we are more energized by negative emotions. They continue to feed us negative news because they know it drives attention. For example, recent research has found that negative words in news headlines increase consumption rates and clicks, while positive words decrease them.

The good news for humanity is that many people are gradually tuning out the negativity and avoiding the news by deleting apps and canceling cable TV subscriptions. I am one of those people who have made a conscious decision in the last five years to reduce my news consumption: I remain well-informed by reading major headlines once a day from a couple of trusted sources, but I don't need to be aware of every single bit of breaking news as it happens. This has definitely made me less anxious, more trusting of others, and more content.

THE NEGATIVE EFFECT of fear is very powerful. My friend Gurmeet and his family are practicing Sikhs who wear turbans when they are in public. In the past, when they went out to have dinner at a restaurant, people would look at them with intrigue and curiosity. Strangers gave them the benefit of the doubt, seeing them as different and interesting; some even asked them about their turbans and what they signified. After 9/11, however, people saw images of Osama bin Laden on TV and started to associate turbans with terrorism and danger. This increased their fear and mistrust. So now when Gurmeet and his family are out having dinner, people become anxious around them. Most try to avoid them, and a few even insult them and tell them to "go back to your country." (The whole family was born in the US.) They are still the same peaceful family, but fear has tainted people's perception of them. While the negative sentiments did settle down a few years after 2001, Gurmeet shared with me that it has actually become even worse in the last few years, due to negative rhetoric against Muslims and immigrants.

This leads to an important point about the feedback effect of fear. Although the world is generally safer, it is not safer for everyone, because so many of us are becoming more fearful. People belonging to racial minorities are still subject to racism, discrimination, and brutality. Which means their reluctance to assume positive intent is totally reasonable and understandable, as we have seen.

Not only does fear cause us to assume negative intentions in the first place, it also prevents us from asking clarifying questions and checking reality with the other person. In his seminal book *The Four Agreements*, the Mexican philosopher don Miguel Ruiz explains how fear and lack of courage are at the core of the assumptions we make:

> Because we are afraid to ask for clarification, we make assumptions, and believe we are right about the assumptions; then we defend our assumptions and try to make someone else wrong. If others tell us something, we make assumptions, and if they don't tell us something, we make assumptions to fulfill our need to know and to replace the need to communicate. Even if we hear something and we don't understand, we make assumptions about what it means and then believe the assumptions. We make all sorts of assumptions because we don't have the courage to ask questions.

To assume positive intention and ask clarifying questions, we need to acknowledge our fears and act despite them. The key obstacle to this is that with fear hardwired in our brain, it has created a cognitive bias called the fundamental attribution error.

Every time we observe someone engaging in an action, there are a couple of tensions going on under the surface in our brains. The first tension is between the action and the intention behind it. The second is between the person (their personality and attributes) and the situation they found themselves in. Psychologists have shown that we are inclined to focus too much on the actions of others and their impact on us, without giving much thought to the possible intentions. That is the fundamental attribution error.

So in that moment when Tim received his coffee, all I could think about was that he had had it delivered to the conference room (the action) and how that had affected my presentation (the impact). I didn't have the presence of mind to pause, just for a moment, and think, "There must be a logical explanation for this. What is his intention?" Moreover, I automatically assumed that Tim's action was due to his personality: He must be selfish, inconsiderate, and entitled. But I didn't think about what may have led to what happened (which in fact was Daniela deciding to bring him the coffee to repay his kindness).

The interaction between a person and the situations they encounter has been studied in depth in the psychological literature. In a well-known study involving students at a religious seminary, researchers asked the students to walk across campus to deliver a sermon to a group. On their way they would come across a man slumped in a doorway and asking for help. The researchers wanted to find out which students would stop to help and which would continue on their way. Most of us would predict that if the student is compassionate and helpful by nature, they are more likely to stop and help than others. In other words, we would expect the student's personality to be the most important predictor of whether they help or not.

The researchers tested that hypothesis by manipulating the experiment: Half of the students were given only five minutes to get to the sermon, and the other half did not have any time limit. For the students in a hurry, only about 10 percent stopped to help the man. For those who were given plenty of time, 63 percent stopped to help. So, stopping or not was mostly related to their situation, not their personality: Were they in a hurry or not when they saw the man in need?

In another study, participants read a scenario that is closely related to our professional lives:

> Ron was a bit late to work on Monday morning because there was a bad traffic jam. When he arrived at work he didn't feel very well and got a slow start on his work for the day. He made it to his 10:00 a.m. staff meeting, but because that meeting ran 10 minutes late, he arrived late at his 11:30 a.m. sales team meeting. At that meeting Ron and three of his coworkers were supposed to present a new production line to the Director, but the presentation wasn't finished and the laptop projector wasn't functioning properly. At 2:30 p.m. when Ron was

back at his desk, three clients called and canceled their long-standing monthly supply contracts with Ron's firm. At 4:00 p.m. Ron was called in to the Director's office and fired.

Ask yourself, What contributed to Ron's firing? His skills, personality, and abilities, or situational factors such as the workplace environment, coworkers, staff, clients, the director, the traffic jam, and work technology? How much weight would you put on each factor? According to research, most people put more blame on Ron himself than on the situation he found himself in. However, after they listened to a lecture about the fundamental attribution error or watched a video related to the importance of situations, they gave less importance to his personality and skills and more to the situation.

If we dig a bit deeper into our brain physiology, it is easy to understand why we fall into these traps. Recent research using brain scanning technology has shown that we spend about 47 percent of our awake time thinking about ourselves, in an aimless way. When we are not actively engaging in intentional mental activity, our brain naturally slides into something called the default mode network (DMN). When the DMN takes over, we only focus on ourselves, and we get increasingly worried and unhappy. We see the world only from our own perspective and don't put ourselves in the shoes of others. Many experts believe that the DMN is where our egos reside.

In essence, the fundamental attribution error exists because of how we perceive the world. While we have at least some idea about our own character and motivations, we rarely know anything about what is going on with someone else. So, thanks to the DMN and our self-protective instincts, we regularly cut ourselves some slack, while holding others totally accountable for their actions. We focus on others' actions and not their intentions, but when we are evaluating ourselves, we do the opposite: We overemphasize our intentions, believing that our mistakes have nothing to do with our personality and everything to do with situations that we have no control over. I don't cut people off on the highway because I am jerk; I do it because I have a doctor's appointment I need to get to. I didn't walk into the meeting 15 minutes late because I am not professional; there was heavy traffic and I just didn't have a choice.

We readily make ourselves the hero of our world and others the villains. And in the process, we suffer in our minds. But we can rewrite this story to a happier one.

— 3 —

How Accountable Positivity Works

DR. VICKY, a physician leader I once worked with, specializes in obstetrics and gynecology. Dr. Vicky and her CEO had a difficult relationship. Somehow, they had started on the wrong foot, mistrusting each other, and things between them kept on getting worse. That vicious cycle went on for years, each one assuming negative intentions in the other and interpreting their actions as malicious.

One day, Dr. Vicky delivered a child whose parents wanted to put him up for adoption. Dr. Vicky was aware that her boss's daughter had been trying to conceive for years but hadn't been able to and was looking to adopt a child. She had heard from others that this issue had caused the boss and her daughter a lot of pain. In a moment of compassion, Dr. Vicky somehow made herself think about her boss as a human being and not as a mean boss. She called her and told her about the baby. The boss was ecstatic and accepted Dr. Vicky's offer to meet the biological parents. After the parents met and filled out the necessary paperwork, the boss's daughter adopted the child.

The relationship between Dr. Vicky and her boss took a 180-degree turn. All of a sudden, the boss started seeing her in a different light, as someone who is compassionate and thoughtful. And Dr. Vicky started to trust the boss more. As soon as they changed their assumptions about each other, a virtuous Cycle of Trust was created, and each subsequent positive interaction served to feed that cycle. They were still the same people who had fought each other tooth and nail in the past, but positive intentions and trust now made them see each other more appreciatively.

YOU MAY be skeptical about the benefits of assuming positive intentions—and justifiably so, because there certainly are situations where you need to protect yourself. You need a pragmatic and flexible mindset, and we'll spend time on that in chapter 4. But let's first get into the details of why you're better off going with the positive until you have a solid reason not to.

Let's start with a practical definition of assuming positive intentions. When someone appears to do something that is wrong, offensive, or unexplainable, assuming positive intentions is about replacing judgment with curiosity. It is about giving the other person the benefit of the doubt and starting with the assumption that the other person has a good reason for acting that way. The research shows that its benefits are both external (a better relationship with that person) and internal (inner calm and happiness).

The external benefits are numerous, especially in a work context, where the importance of relationships cannot be overemphasized. The evidence suggests that when relationships among team members are strong and collaborative, employee retention and engagement are improved, innovation is sparked, and productivity is increased. Moreover, burnout is reduced while employee well-being and career success improve as well. Approaching all work relationships with a positive mindset can improve decisions, build productive collaborations, and strengthen trust.

This means starting with this mindset before the interaction has taken place, and even before the other person has done anything positive or negative. The idea is to act under the assumption that the colleague is trustworthy and that they share our desire for a positive outcome for the team, and to expect them to behave in a positive way—even if we don't know that for sure yet. When that is our starting point, our body relaxes, and what we say and how we act towards them automatically becomes more open and positive. As we interact with them, we look for messages that validate our positive assumptions (and ignore the ones that don't) to reduce cognitive dissonance in our minds. In contrast, if we had started with assuming negative intentions, we would have looked for signs that the other person is not trustworthy, and most likely we would have found them in what they say and how they act.

How do positive intentions impact trust? So often when we think of whether to trust, we see it as something external that is forced on us: "I have no choice but to mistrust this person." But that is not always true; trust is a choice we make. By changing our assumptions towards others, we can choose to trust (or mistrust) them.

If that sounds unrealistic to you, let's do a thought experiment that I learned from psychologist and teamwork expert Dr. Liane Davey. Think of a colleague at work that you trust completely and with no reservations. Now imagine that they did something negative towards you, such as leaving you out of an important meeting. You would be hurt by their decision, but you are likely to rationalize it and think to yourself, "I am sure they didn't mean to hurt me—they must have had a good reason. I'd better go check with them."

Now think of a colleague that you totally mistrust. Imagine that one day they offer to help you on an important project with a tight deadline. You will probably find a way to interpret their behavior in a negative way. You might say to yourself, "They only offered to help so they can appear like a team player in front of the boss" or "They must have a hidden agenda; they are definitely planning to sabotage my project and make me look bad." Chances are you are going to believe these assumptions and decline their offer for help.

When we start with assuming good intentions, we act more positively and openly with the other person, and they are more likely to respond in the same way, creating a virtuous Cycle of Trust. Positivity begets positivity. Openness begets openness. It creates reciprocity in our relationships, which can be a game changer.

The research shows that high-performing teams do not leave trust up to chance or to random moments of compassion. They take the initiative to proactively resolve conflicts and tension. In those teams, colleagues are interested in hearing if they upset a teammate and are willing to reach out if they've done so. They adopt a "growth mindset" towards relationships by believing that while they have their ups and downs, they can always be repaired. This mindset of checking with others and believing that relationships can be improved is at the core of assuming positive intentions.

WE CAN LOOK at the effects of this in team leadership in terms of two opposite cycles: the Cycle of Mistrust and the Cycle of Trust. I'll illustrate the Cycle of Mistrust with Salim, a leader who has had many negative experiences with team members.

1. Salim takes on a new job and joins his team already predisposed to making *negative assumptions* about their intentions.

2. These beliefs cause Salim to act in *self-protective* ways to defend himself against potential harm from his team members.

3. As a result, Salim starts acting in *aggressive* ways towards them.

4. In return, the team members naturally interpret Salim's behavior in a negative way and start assuming the worst about *his* intentions.

5. They then act in self-protective ways of their own to defend themselves against Salim.
6. Before too long, they start acting aggressively towards him.
7. This confirms Salim's original suspicion about them, and the cycle repeats itself.

The Cycle of Mistrust
(adapted from Ryan and Oestreich)

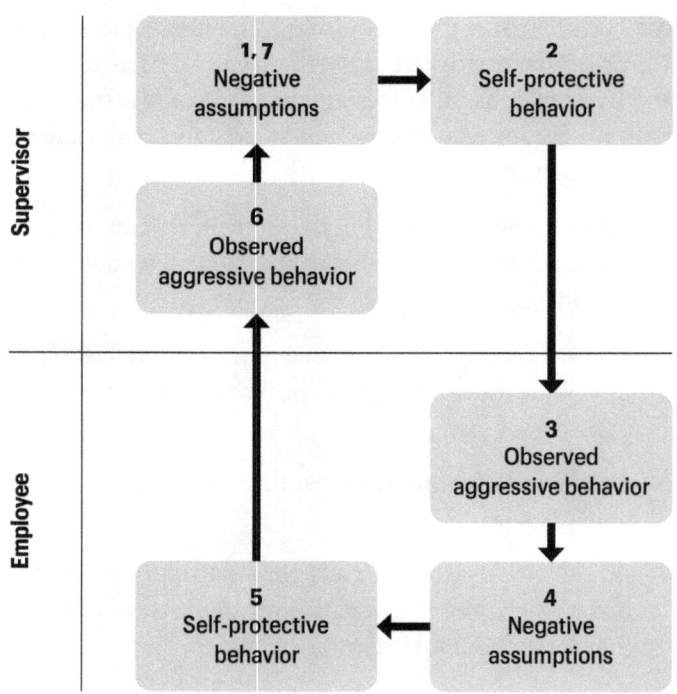

Examples of negative assumptions that some leaders make are that employees are not accountable, do not really care about their work beyond getting a paycheck, look for excuses, and resist changes that are beneficial for the organization. Because of these assumptions, leaders then engage in self-protective strategies such as micromanaging, developing tighter rules, limiting the information communicated to employees, and emphasizing the formal chain of command. From the employee's perspective, these strategies appear to have been implemented without any logical reasons. They start seeing two sets of rules, one for managers and one for employees. They become more suspicious of closed-door meetings, and rumors about possible layoffs or reorganizations start to spread.

The employees then start to assume that the leaders are insensitive to their needs, secretive about decisions, only interested in power and control, and continuously try to get more work out of them with no additional rewards. These assumptions lead employees to prevent information from flowing up the organization, take pleasure in seeing a leader make a wrong decision, make fun of and gossip about leaders behind their backs, and refuse to contribute in meetings (but complain about them afterwards). In turn, leaders see these self-protective strategies as evidence of incompetence, whining, and resistance to change, and the cycle continues.

This is clearly a destructive cycle—and the way to break it is through assuming positive intentions. If Salim can somehow shift his mindset and start with a blank slate of positive or even neutral assumptions, things can change. While there are significant forces that predisposed him to assume negative intentions and mistrust others (we will discuss these in the next chapter), they are not insurmountable. He can change his mindset, shift his assumptions, and behave differently. Here's how he can make the Cycle of Trust work:

1. Salim starts with the assumption that employees generally want to do a good job and are intrinsically honest and trustworthy.

2. He then treats his employees with kindness and trust.

3. The employees see this treatment and appreciate it.

4. They assume that he wants the workload to be fair and reasonable and that he wants their inputs on decisions.

And stages 5, 6, and 7 of the Cycle of Trust follow. The Cycle of Mistrust is broken, and instead trust starts to develop. Both parties extend the most generous interpretation to the intentions, words, and actions of the other.

The Cycle of Trust
(adapted from Ryan and Oestreich)

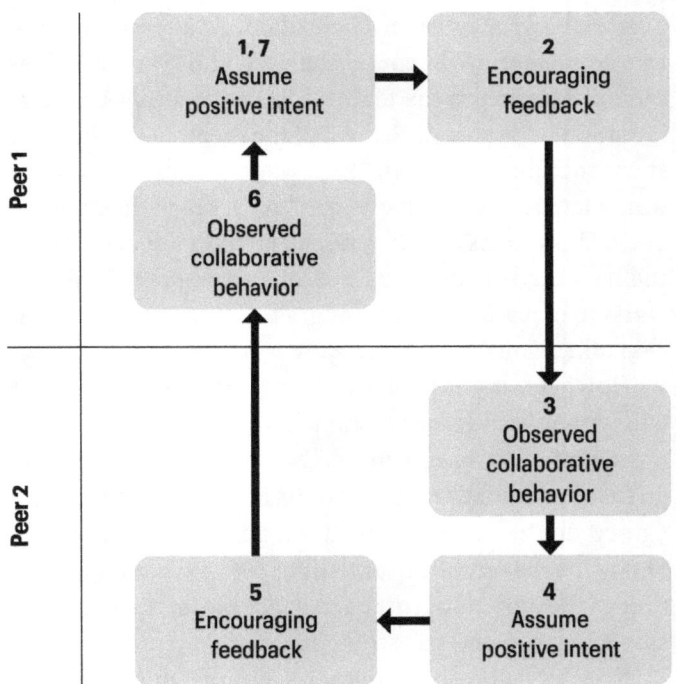

ONE OF THE BEST leadership coaches I know is Tom Henschel. Tom has been working with leaders for decades and has also hosted a podcast about executive coaching since 2006 (way before podcasts were a thing). Tom told me he has experienced numerous work situations where positive or negative intentions played a crucial role.

He shared a potential scenario involving two colleagues he worked with. Seong and Sam, both directors, have agreed not to share an important piece of information with anyone else on their team. At a team meeting, the conversation becomes heated and Sam divulges the information to the team. If Seong assumes negative intentions, she spends the rest of the meeting fuming. She starts thinking to herself, "Sam wants to sabotage me; he wants to put himself above me." As soon as the meeting ends, she storms into his office and asks angrily, "What the hell, man? Didn't we have an agreement?" When he starts to explain, she is too angry to listen. Their relationship takes a hit and may never recover.

However, if Seong assumes positive intentions, she will withhold judgment. She will think to herself, "Sam must have something in mind." After the meeting, she will go to him without preconceptions and say, "I thought we agreed not to share. How did we get our wires crossed?" She will listen carefully as Sam explains what happened. And as they learn to trust each other more, their relationship may even become stronger.

Now let's consider another scenario, this one in an employer-employee dynamic. Anita has been coming to work late for the last few weeks. If her boss, Natalie, assumes Anita has negative intentions, she thinks to herself, "This Anita is a hot mess. She can't even self-regulate!" She confronts her with judgment and irritation. She doesn't listen to Anita's explanations, and she doesn't give her any wiggle room.

However, if Natalie assumes positive intentions, she is more likely to think about the cause: "What could be causing Anita to be late? I know she is a single parent, and she has an old car. I think I'll ask her about that." Natalie will have a conversation about punctuality with Anita and hold her accountable for her actions, but it is a conversation that comes from a place of curiosity and understanding.

When assuming positive intentions is intentionally and repeatedly implemented within an organization, it becomes part of the culture and people start thinking about it as "the way we do things around here." That is exactly what happened at Erin Wade's restaurant. Wade started her career in law and was working for a prestigious law firm. But she did not enjoy her job or the people she worked with. One time, after another long and miserable workday, she came home craving a good bowl of macaroni and cheese. Her father had always made her mac and cheese when she was a child and was having a tough day. However, she found out it wasn't available at the restaurants in her area. That planted a seed, and after much thinking and planning, she decided to quit her legal job and start Homeroom, a restaurant that served only mac and cheese using her father's old recipe.

While the food was certainly wonderful, it was not the reason Homeroom became one of the best and most profitable restaurants in the country. It was the culture that Wade created that made the difference, one that treated employees like adults and assumed their intentions were positive. For example, Wade and her team practiced open-book management: Everyone in the restaurant, including waitstaff and dishwashers, had access to all the financials and were actively engaged in major decisions on the operations and strategy of the restaurant.

Another revolutionary concept that Wade implemented was the use of restorative justice in holding staff accountable. In most restaurants and workplaces, staff that are late for work get written up or have their pay docked. But Wade noticed that this approach did not work: Homeroom's staff kept on coming in late no matter how much punishment she dished out. So, she decided to try an approach based on restorative justice: If you do something wrong, you have to apologize and make it right to the people who were negatively affected by your actions. Waiters who came in late had to apologize to their coworkers who had to pick up the slack when they were late and to the customers who didn't get their food on time because there weren't enough waitstaff. As a result of this change, waiters started to understand how their lateness hurt others. They didn't want to let their coworkers and customers down. Lateness was significantly reduced.

The culture at Homeroom may be that of a small specialty restaurant, but many of its principles are universal and can be implemented in most industries. And to do this effectively, remember that assuming positive intent does not mean we focus on intent and ignore the impact. On the contrary, it requires us to take responsibility for the impact of our words and actions and to hold others accountable for theirs. Giving people the benefit of the doubt does not replace conflict management and having difficult conversations. It is a prerequisite that makes sure we enter these conversations with the right mindset. When someone misbehaves, whether intentionally or not, we make them aware of the situation and the impact of their actions on us, and we give them the opportunity to explain their behavior and correct it in the future. In this approach, assuming positive intentions is complemented by owning the impacts of actions on others: accountable positivity. And, as we'll see in the next chapter, it shows us the limits that accountability imposes.

— 4 —

The Limits

A WHILE AGO, I became acquainted with the father of a boy who went to school with my children. We would talk to each other when we waited for the kids to come out of school and at school events. The following year his son left the school, and for a while I lost touch with them. A couple of years later, I got a text message from the father asking if we could talk on the phone. We arranged a time and he shared that due to health problems, their family, was enduring some serious financial difficulties. He asked if he could borrow some money. I was a bit surprised by the request, as our relationship was not that close. I told him I would think about it. They were a decent family, and I liked them. I reasoned that for him to ask for a loan from someone he didn't know that well clearly meant that he needed the money. I assumed positive intent. I told him it would be my pleasure to lend him the money. He was very appreciative and promised he would pay it back in three weeks when he got paid.

You may have guessed how the rest of the story goes. I didn't get the money in three weeks or even three months.

It took almost a year, and countless text messages, to finally get the money back. The experience left a bad taste in my mouth and made me decide to never lend money to anyone again. If in future a friend or relative needs financial help, I will give it as a gift without any expectation of payback.

THIS IS WHERE we face the risks and reach the limits of assuming positive intention and why positivity must be accountable. In my work with leaders, I have heard numerous stories of executives getting burned when they assumed the best. A new clinical leader in a hospital assumed positive intent when one of his clinicians made a mistake in diagnosing a patient. He gave the clinician the benefit of the doubt and assumed the mistake was due to overwork. It turned out the clinician had a history of making similar mistakes due to negligence. The leader appeared very naïve in front of other executives and vowed to be more careful in the future.

At another organization, a vice president confidentially shared some sensitive information with a colleague about her plans for expanding a product line. The colleague betrayed the trust and shared the information with other executives. This led to serious questioning of the vice president's "aggressive ambitions" and whether she was a team player. She was deeply hurt and became very cautious when sharing information with colleagues.

The limits can also show up in smaller ways. Sometimes another person does something that annoys, offends, or harms us, but we don't do anything about it because we are conflict-averse and convince ourselves that "it's not a big deal"—and then the other person repeats the offense, and we are left feeling helpless and angry. "Sure, it is usually good to assume that the other person had positive intent," notes professor Jim Detert, the author of the influential book *Choosing Courage*. "But often telling yourself 'it's not a big deal' (perhaps including 'because they meant well') is a cognitive distortion that serves the short-term purpose of forgoing a difficult conversation or action while setting you up for bigger problems down the road."

There is clearly a point beyond which giving the benefit of the doubt becomes an ineffective strategy that leads to a person being perceived as a pushover. When we assume positive intent, we still have to find the courage to have the difficult conversation and test the reality—which will be the subject of chapter 9.

There are also other serious limitations to assuming positive intentions, especially when it comes to race relations. In chapter 1, I shared an example of a person of color assuming positive intent in a white person and how that led to a better outcome in that instance. But certainly, people belonging to marginalized groups should not be burdened with always assuming positive intentions. My friend and colleague Dr. Deneese Jones, a retired academic leader and African American woman, explained to me that for most people of color, trust doesn't come easily. Their life experiences of being marginalized and discriminated against—intentionally or unintentionally—have naturally predisposed them to have their guard up and withhold trust until it is earned. For them, assuming positive intent is a calculated risk.

Ruth Terry, a Black and Latina journalist, offers a similar perspective. She tells the story of an ongoing dispute she had with her white neighbor Kathy. In the apartment building where they lived, Kathy was known as a problematic neighbor that everyone tried to accommodate. People avoided the laundry room on "Kathy's day" and kept their pets quiet so that Kathy wasn't provoked. But Kathy didn't reciprocate the considerate behavior: She often engaged in loud arguments in her apartment at various times of the day and night.

One day, Ruth wanted to record an important interview in her apartment, so she kindly asked Kathy to keep the noise level down. Kathy responded angrily to the request and stormed into Ruth's apartment to yell at her in her own kitchen. Hurt and irritated, Ruth went to talk to a white friend to vent. The friend advised Ruth to assume positive intent and give Kathy the benefit of the doubt. Ruth was not happy with the advice: "Assuming Kathy's positive intent felt like letting her off the hook. And deep down, I resented that my white friend was asking me, the only Black woman in our neighborhood, to assume positive intent behind the actions of a privileged white woman with anger management problems. If I acted like Kathy, would anyone assume my positive intent? It's doubtful."

One reason why assuming positive intent is not beneficial in these situations is that it ignores the impact. We can't always let people off the hook because their intent may not have been negative. If you accidentally break an expensive plate in your friend's house, the plate is still broken and you still have to pay for it. Lena Tenney, the coordinator of public engagement at the Kirwan Institute for the Study of Race and Ethnicity at Ohio State University, explains the difference: "All of this focus on intention essentially remarginalizes a person of color who's speaking up about racism by telling them that their experience doesn't matter because the person didn't mean it that way."

In Ruth's case, Kathy's outburst in her kitchen five minutes before she was due to record an interview didn't just lead to a distracted interview but also triggered panic attacks for a long time after. Kathy's intent didn't matter, even if it could have been positive somehow, because the accumulated impact of her negative actions was significant to Ruth. In those types of situations, giving the benefit of the doubt and getting it from others appear to be a privilege that traditionally dominant groups have, while more marginalized groups don't.

Another way that assuming positive intentions can be used negatively in race relations at work is when it is applied only to people in in-groups. With the progress achieved by DEI (diversity, equity and inclusion) efforts in most organizations, blatant discrimination against marginalized people has decreased. However, positive discrimination in favor of in-group people—whether intentional or not—is still very prevalent. This often takes the form of giving the benefit of the doubt selectively. For example, when a white job applicant doesn't have a good interview, a white interviewer might think, "Maybe he didn't mean to say that." If the applicant arrived late, the interviewer might assume, "She probably had a valid reason." But the interviewer might not extend the same benefit of the doubt to someone who isn't white.

For these and other reasons, some people have pushed against the idea of assuming positive intent because they perceive it as ignoring the impact of actions and disregarding accountability, leading to toxic positivity, as I discussed in chapter 1. And indeed it does carry the risk of giving people a pass on their bad behaviors when harmful incidents are swept under the rug, emotions and experiences are invalidated, victims are blamed, and accountability is sidestepped.

But in my decades of studying positive psychology and the science of trust, humility, and accountability, I have seen that this doesn't have to be the case. If we can learn to assume positive intent appropriately and follow it up with difficult conversations, it results not in toxic positivity but in trust, collaboration, and peace of mind. We just need to recognize that assuming positive intentions is not enough by itself. It has to be coupled with accountability.

When someone lets us down or wrongs us, we provisionally give them the benefit of the doubt, *and* we verify their intent. We make them aware of their action and its impact, and we hold them accountable when appropriate. I like to call this "API & Verify": we *assume positive intentions*, and we *verify* that they actually have them. This is the core of accountable positivity, and I will be showing in detail how to practice it in chapters 5 through 10.

IT IS, of course, especially difficult to assume positive intentions with someone you have not worked with before. With people we know, we typically decide whether to trust them based on two factors: their character and their competence. We trust them because they tell the truth and do what they say they're going to do (character), or because they have the skills to do the work and a track record of having done it before (competence). But with a new colleague, we are asking ourselves to trust without the benefit of all that prior information. Jump, and then hope that solid ground will appear. Which is obviously very risky.

Will everyone live up to that trust? Of course not. Based on my experience working with hundreds of leaders and graduate students, I estimate that about 3 percent of people are rotten or incompetent and do not deserve that trust. These are the people who will try to take full advantage of us, every single time. Others may say I am naïve and that the actual number is closer to 5 percent or even 10. We each have our own experiences. But even if it is 10 percent, I would argue that the benefits of assuming positive intent in the other 90 percent of situations far outweigh the negatives of being taken advantage of by the minority. As I maintain throughout this book, this approach is much more likely to lead to productive relationships, and it makes us happier and more at peace. When I start my day thinking that everyone is trying their best, it is a much more positive frame of mind. Instead of spending my time thinking about how other people are trying to take advantage of me, I focus my attention on more important stuff.

Still, some people will question even the 10 percent estimate because it implies that most people are decent and well-meaning, and only a small minority are not. What is the evidence for that?

The evidence is in fact overwhelming, from psychology, biology, archaeology, anthropology, sociology, and history, that "most people, deep down, are pretty decent." In his brilliant and evidence-based book *Humankind*, the Dutch author Rutger Bregman presents the following scenario:

> Imagine an airplane makes an emergency landing and breaks into three parts. As the cabin fills with smoke, everybody inside realizes: We've got to get out of here. What happens?
>
> - On Planet A, the passengers turn to their neighbors to ask if they're okay. Those needing assistance are helped out of the plane first. People are willing to give their lives, even for perfect strangers.
>
> - On Planet B, everyone's left to fend for themselves. Panic breaks out. There's lots of pushing and shoving. Children, the elderly, and people with disabilities get trampled underfoot.
>
> Now the question: Which planet do we live on?

Most people would say we live on Planet B. But in fact, all the scientific evidence from prehistory till today suggests that we actually live on Planet A. Crisis after crisis all over the world has shown that when human beings face difficulties, they actually become kinder towards each other, not meaner. And that is why we are better off assuming positive intentions.

Bregman offers a practical argument for assuming positive intent: "If you decide not to trust someone, you'll never know if you're right. Because you'll never get any feedback. Let's say you get screwed over by some blond Dutch guy, so you swear never again to trust blond people from Holland. For the rest of your life, you'll be suspicious of all blond Dutchies, without ever having to face the simple truth that most of them are pretty decent." The research confirms Bregman's point: People who are more trusting get to interact with a far bigger range of humans than non-trusting people. They do tend to get lied to more, but they also become better at detecting lies because of their wide experiences.

In my conversations with numerous people while writing this book, some of them asked, "What about con artists?" One even suggested that con artists are going to love my book because it will convince people to be more gullible, making them easier to take advantage of. To answer that question, I turned to the expert on fraudsters, psychologist Maria Konnikova. Konnikova has studied con artists throughout her career, so we might expect her to advise us to be cautious and assume negative intent to protect ourselves. But instead she recommends that we make peace with the fact that we will occasionally be taken advantage of and cheated. "That's a small price to pay for the luxury of a lifetime of trusting other people," Bregman agrees.

Years ago I was preparing to attend an academic conference, and to save on cost, a friend of mine and I decided to share a hotel room. One morning as we were getting ready to leave the room, my friend strongly advised that I not leave my half-full bottle of water in the room. Surprised, I asked him why. He said the hotel cleaning staff will surely spit in it when they come to service our room. I was confused—why would they do that? I had never thought of that possibility, but my friend was certain that it happens all the time.

We clearly had different perspectives on life. He believed that people will try to harm you for no reason, but I argued that if everyone thought like this, society couldn't function. No one would ever order a drink or a meal at a restaurant or interact with a stranger for any reason. My friend was not convinced.

I prefer my perspective. It's a better way to live and work.

— 5 —

Making It Work

IN HIS EXCELLENT BOOK *Be Where Your Feet Are*, Scott O'Neil tells the story of the city of Camden, New Jersey. At one point in time, Camden was the most dangerous city in the US, riddled with rampant crime, drug use, and terrifying neighborhoods that kept scared families cooped up in their small homes. Camden's police department was well trained and competent, but no matter what they did, crime and drug use kept on increasing.

One hot summer day in 2013, a local gang went on a shooting spree and killed three members of a rival gang, an incident that unfortunately was all too common in Camden. Police chief Scott Thomson quickly got together with his team to plan a response. They wanted to do what they always did in this situation: flood the neighborhood with heavily armed SWAT teams and hope to get some information from scared neighbors about who was responsible for the shooting.

But there was one problem with this approach: Chief Thomson knew it wouldn't work. They'd been trying such tactics for years with no effect. After a bit of thinking, he had a new idea: "What if we change our mindset? What if, instead of assuming that everyone in the neighborhood is a criminal and should be arrested, we assume positive intention and show up in a friendlier way to build trust with the community?" His team members were very skeptical, but they were desperate. So, they decided to give the new approach a try.

Thomson located two ice cream trucks, told them to stop at the two corners of the street where the shooting happened, and paid them to hand free ice cream cones to everyone who showed up. When the ice cream trucks appeared on the street, the residents were still shaken up from the shootings and were hiding inside their homes. But as soon as the neighborhood kids heard the music from the trucks, they started begging their parents to let them out. A few parents finally relented and went out carefully with their kids, and to their surprise they found members of the police, unarmed, handing out free ice cream. Before too long, everyone was out on the street.

On that day the residents and police in Camden did something they'd never done before: They talked with each other and actually had a good time. In no time, the residents started to offer tips on the shooting, and the following day the police swiftly arrested the suspects without a single shot being fired. The Camden police department has since adopted assuming positive intentions as its main approach to working with the community. And in return, the community started to trust the police and volunteer information about who was causing trouble. More and more neighbors sat outside on their front porches while the kids rode their bikes on the sidewalks. They claimed their streets back from the gangs. And Camden became one of the safest cities in the US, with some of the lowest arrest rates and highest high school graduation rates. That is the power of assuming positive intentions—because positivity begets positivity, it can create cultures of trust and repair entire communities.

APPLYING THE CAMDEN POLICE approach to other communities is not always straightforward, though. Community-oriented policing, as it is commonly referred to, has been implemented in many cities and yet trust in law enforcement has remained low. Researchers David Yeager, Kyle Dobson, and Andrea Dittman wanted to understand the reasons, so they studied 233 instances in which police officers interacted with community members. In some of these exchanges, the public felt threatened and annoyed that the police just came up to them and started asking them questions while they were trying to have a nice day at the park with their families. However, in other interactions, the conversation went very well and the public felt more trustful of the police officers.

What made the difference? The researchers found that in the second group, the police officers started by explaining their intent. When they approached the families at the park, they started with a "transparency statement": "I'm walking around trying to get to know the community." This statement signaled to the community members that the police had positive intentions, and as a result they felt more relaxed and more trustful of the police. In this instance, the police officers did not just assume the positive intentions of the residents; they also projected their own positivity when they interacted with them.

Transparency statements are now being used by police officers all around the country, and their applications have expanded to include all types of organizations. For example, before a manager rounds on their team members, they explain to them, "I am raising this so I can better understand your work and how I can support you better." This ensures that the team member doesn't assume that the manager is there to spy on them. Similarly, a school principal may say to a struggling teacher, "I would like to sit in on your class so I can understand what you need and you can be more successful." The teacher is less likely to think that they are in trouble or being monitored for poor performance.

My colleague Dr. Kyle Rickner, a family physician, told me about how he assumes positive intentions with new patients. Patients in the US, especially those that are uninsured or come from a low socioeconomic status, tend to view the healthcare system as one that consistently mistreats and cheats them. They are suspicious of hospitals and clinics, and they don't trust doctors. In return, many doctors don't trust these patients and assume that many of them lie about their conditions to get pain medications to fuel their addictions. Dr. Rickner attempts to break the cycle by projecting positivity and assuming positive intention in his patients. In his first encounter with them, he listens intently and treats them with benevolence. And almost instantly, they drop their guard and engage with him so that he can help them address their problems.

Author and activist Simran Jeet Singh shares a telling experience. In his excellent book *The Light We Give*, Simran—a devout Sikh—talks about the importance of compassion, even towards people who have wronged us. Compassion, according to Simran, is based on curiosity and courage. Curiosity is the opposite of judgment; it allows us to see the other person's humanity. But curiosity is useless unless we act on it. And to do that, we need courage to connect with other people and have a conversation with them.

As a practicing Sikh, Simran wears a turban every day, which makes some people associate him with the appearance of some terrorists. In one interview, he related the story of a time when he was jogging in New York City:

> As I'm running I hear someone shouting at me, "f—ing Osama, f—ing Osama." I could have ignored it and just felt irritated. But as I'm running by, I look at this person and he's probably 18 or 20 years old, the same age as my students. So I stopped and I went up to him. He waved me off like he wanted to dismiss me, and I said, "No, actually we're going to have a little conversation about this." He was a person of color, and I said, "I'm guessing you know what it's like for people to say these kinds of things to you, how hurtful it can be." And I saw his eyes change, from distance to sincerity. We shook hands, and I went on with my run. And it's not that I feel

like I changed the world in that moment, but it totally changed my day and it changed the way I try to handle situations like that when it's appropriate.

Instead of suffering in silence, Simran chose to see the humanity of the other person and actually talk to him. This seemed to have an impact on the young man, and it definitely made Simran feel better as he continued his run. Again, not every person being subjected to a racist slur is expected to act like Simran did. But it is important to acknowledge it as an option.

At a recent talk that Simran gave, I asked him about how he convinces people to act this way. He said he tells them that behaving with compassion is the right thing to do, it makes other people's lives better, and most importantly it makes their own lives better.

WE MAY THINK that the most obvious question in deciding whether to assume positive intentions is whether we are dealing with someone we know, such as a family member or a friend, or a complete stranger. At Trinity University, we did a survey of about 200 professionals and graduate students that showed something different, though. We asked respondents to reflect on various scenarios related to family members, friends, colleagues, and total strangers. The results showed that people's choices to assume positive or negative intent were not just related to whether they knew the other person or not. They were more related to the specific situation and relationship and to the severity of the other person's behavior. Here is a breakdown of the various scenarios with the percentage of people who selected the interpretation that assumes positive intent (API).

People We Know Well

Significant other: You call your significant other during the workday to ask for some information, and they answer you in a curt way and then hang up quickly.
- Positive interpretation: "They must have been in the middle of something important."
- API: 83.6%

Boss: You hand your boss the report they asked for. They frown and barely acknowledge it.
- Positive interpretation: "They have so much on their mind."
- API: 53.3%

Friend: You send a text to your friend asking if they want to get together on the weekend. It takes them a full day to answer back and then they say they can't make it.
- Positive interpretation: "They are probably busy with work and family."
- API: 88.7%

Direct report: Your direct report sends you a large Excel sheet with a significant mistake in it.
- Positive interpretation: "I wonder if they were distracted or maybe need some Excel training."
- API: 93.3%

People We Don't Know Well

New colleague: Your new colleague is 15 minutes late for an important meeting.
- Positive interpretation: "They must have been delayed by a valid reason."
- API: 62.5%

Driver: A driver cuts you off on the highway.
- Positive interpretation: "This person must be late for an important appointment."
- API: 15.9%

Traveler: The person in front of you at the security line at the airport is taking too long to remove their electronics from their bag.
- Positive interpretation: "Traveling is stressful for everyone."
- API: 75.4%

Audience member: You're giving an important presentation at a conference, and a person sitting in the front row is preoccupied with their phone. Ten minutes later they stand up and walk out of the room.

- Positive interpretation: "They must have received an important text and they need to make a call."
- API: 81.5%

Client: You make a mistake while working with a client and send a long apology email. You don't hear anything back.

- Positive interpretation: "They are so busy, they must have moved on."
- API: 46.1%

Blind date: The other person texts 30 minutes before the date to say they can't make it and would like to reschedule.

- Positive interpretation: "They must have had an emergency come up."
- API: 47.7%

Our respondents were more likely to assume positive intent with their significant others, friends, direct reports, travelers, and audience members. They were less likely to do so with their bosses, other drivers, clients, or blind dates.

To make sense of these results, it is important to dive a bit deeper into the science of trust. The latest research shows that trust is very individual: Our personal experiences, more than our genes or upbringing, are a major determinant of whether we trust others or not. It is likely that people don't assume positive intent with a blind date because of negative experiences they've had with previous blind dates. If my first experience with a tall accountant was a negative one, I will hesitate to trust tall accountants in the future. The baggage we carry with us from our own experiences significantly impacts our assumptions.

Moreover, the research shows that when we are interacting face-to-face with another person, we subconsciously judge their trustworthiness based on their facial features. While this is efficient, the evidence suggests that these visual heuristics are neither accurate nor reliable. Our decision whether to trust the stranger in front of us is typically made in 0.25 seconds and is likely to be wrong.

In *Talking to Strangers*, Malcolm Gladwell argues that we are horrible at dealing with strangers face-to-face. We assume we are very good at predicting how people are feeling from their facial expressions, but facial expressions are in fact not very accurate. As a result, we develop inaccurate beliefs about how people truly feel in certain situations, such as after the death of a loved one. And if that belief does not fit with how we expect them to act in that situation, we get confused and make inaccurate judgments ("This person is not acting like someone who has just lost a family member, therefore they must have had something to do with the death"). We assume negative intent when we shouldn't.

Further complications arise when we consider whether we really know our friends or loved ones. Research on empathic accuracy by psychologist William Ickes confirms Gladwell's observations and shows that strangers read each other's thoughts and feelings with an average accuracy of only 20 percent. While that is not very surprising, we would expect that percentage to be much higher for married couples and close friends. But the scientific evidence shows it is not. The average accuracy in reading a spouse or close friend increases by a mere 15 points, reaching only 35 percent. Which means that two times out of three, we are wrong about their intentions. What makes this even more problematic is that most people are way more confident than that in how much they think they know the minds of their spouses and friends, such as their likes and dislikes. This suggests we are not that good at accurately assessing positive or negative intent even with people we know very well.

But at least when we are face-to-face, we have some details that we can't fill in with inaccurate imaginings. Assuming positive intent in an office is very different than in a virtual setting such as Zoom. The number of remote workers has significantly increased since the COVID pandemic, and in workplaces that are fully or partially remote, getting to know your coworkers and develop trust in them can be very hard, given that interactions tend to be limited to virtual calls and meetings. The personal connection and rapport that are typically built in in-person situations—by having lunch together in the break room, chatting in the hallway, or dropping in to someone's office—are very limited in the virtual environment. "Without regular, face-to-face interactions with colleagues, it's harder to pick up on social cues and the nuances of communication, collaboration, and teamwork," notes the journalist and workplace expert Rebecca Knight. Opportunities for misunderstandings that push people to assume negative intentions in each other are much more prevalent.

For example, you share a suggestion during a Zoom meeting and one of your colleagues rolls their eyes. You interpret the eye roll as a sign of passive-aggressiveness directed at you. But in reality, your colleague—sitting in their home office overlooking their front yard—was annoyed that their lawnmowing crew showed up two hours later than usual and are now disturbing their call with the noise. Their eye roll had nothing to do with you, but there is no way for you to know that. So, you inaccurately assume negative intentions.

Given the challenges of the virtual environment, we need to be more intentional about finding one-on-one time with colleagues and direct reports to build trust and alignment with them. Nancy Rothbard, a professor of management at the Wharton School, recommends that you "create common ground and establish shared values; ask questions and seek information that helps you understand their lived experience and circumstances." As a result, shared reality is cultivated where people understand, trust, and assume positive intent. Another suggestion is to work on developing our skills of observation by paying careful attention to our coworkers' facial expressions and vocal tones. We need to watch for how they convey their messages and to learn their nonverbal cues to minimize opportunities for assuming negative intent.

And, at the same time, we need to be conscious of what we don't know. We just aren't as good at judging intentions as we think we are. This is why we need to work to maintain a baseline assumption of positive intentions—because, as we've seen, it's the best strategy. But we still have to do it with our eyes open. Over the next five chapters, we're going to see how to realistically put that into action.

— 6 —

Realistic Optimism

SINCE ASSUMING negative intention is part of our default setting, we need to adopt a new mindset and learn new behaviors to start assuming the opposite. The first aspect is realistic optimism.

Let's say you have a challenging task and want to select applicants that can do it well. First, you will probably assess their talent: Do they have the skills required to do the task? Second, you'll check their motivation: Do they have the desire to put in the effort needed? Most of us would think talent and desire, by themselves, are enough to predict success.

But we are missing something, according to Martin Seligman. Seligman, the father of positive psychology, argues that another crucial factor is optimism. His research over the years has shown that even a person with talent and motivation in abundance may still fail if they lack optimism.

Now, if you have experienced success in the past, of course you tend to be more optimistic. But Seligman shows that people are often successful *because* they are optimistic. Optimistic people succeed in all different areas because they make the most of their talent and persist in the face of both routine setbacks and major failures.

Research in the last 30 years has demonstrated that optimism leads to positive outcomes throughout our personal and professional lives. First of all, it clearly improves our health: Optimistic patients tend to know more about their risk factors and are better able to deal with their health problems practically. Moreover, optimists are less likely to develop chronic conditions and less likely to be readmitted to the hospital after surgery. Cancer patients who are more optimistic feel better about their quality of life and are less distressed.

At work, optimists have more of an intrinsic motivation to work harder and overcome stressful situations. They tend to be happier, more task-oriented, focused on solutions, perseverant, and better at making decisions, which results in more well-being overall. Not surprisingly, optimists are more productive than pessimists and enjoy more career satisfaction and success. A *Harvard Business Review* study of professionals at hundreds of companies across various industries has shown that optimists are 40 percent more likely to get a promotion the following year, six times more likely to be highly engaged in their work, and five times less likely to burn out.

SO, WHAT IS OPTIMISM? Some of us may think of being optimistic as making affirmations to ourselves every morning, such as "You can do this!" But the evidence shows that these statements have little effect on our optimism and success. A beneficial optimism is not about looking at the world with rose-colored glasses and announcing, "Everything is going to be great!" The useful type of optimism is more pragmatic: It takes circumstances and challenges into consideration and still believes that things are going to get better. We call this *realistic optimism*.

The central skill of realistic optimism, Seligman's research suggests, is knowing what to say to ourselves after we experience a setback or failure. Our way of explaining negative events to ourselves determines how helpless or energized we become after these events occur. He describes this explanatory style as the way we reflect "the world in our heart." When a pessimist experiences a setback, they tend to say to themselves, "It's my fault, this bad thing is going to last forever, and it's going to ruin my whole life." A realistic optimist, on the other hand, is likely to interpret the setback like this: "It was just bad luck, this bad thing will go away quickly, and there are other good things in my life that are more important."

Our way of explaining bad events is a habit of thought learned early in life and is derived from how we view our value in the world—whether we think we are worthless and hopeless (pessimism) or valuable and deserving (realistic optimism). The explanatory style can be broken down into three main dimensions:

1. Permanence
2. Pervasiveness
3. Personalization

Let's start with *permanence*. Pessimists tend to give up easily because they believe that setbacks and failures are permanent: They are here to stay and will continue to ruin their lives. Optimists, on the other hand, resist this helplessness and believe that setbacks and failures are temporary, no matter how serious they are. For example, a pessimist having an issue with their boss may think to themselves, "My boss is a jerk; they're just this way and they're never going to change." The realistic optimist may react to the same situation by thinking, "My boss is in a bad mood today; I am sure they will be better tomorrow."

Permanence is about time. *Pervasiveness*, the second dimension, is about space and whether we interpret the setback as specific or universal.

Take the example of two colleagues, Marisela and Marcos, who were both laid off from their jobs. They are both very upset. Marcos starts thinking of himself as a failure and lets the setback affect all other aspects of his life. He neglects his family and stops working out. He spends his days in his sweatpants on the couch. He complains that he will never be able to find another job, so he doesn't try anymore.

Marisela, on the other hand, knows that losing her job is serious, but she doesn't let it affect her personal life. She continues to take care of her family, and she makes a point of maintaining her exercise routine. She takes advantage of the extra time she has to spend more time with her kids and sign up for a yoga class she always thought about. Every morning, she dresses up in a professional way to pursue different job opportunities and prepare for interviews. She believes she is going to find another job soon.

The main difference between Marcos and Marisela is that Marcos catastrophizes, while Marisela compartmentalizes. Marcos lets his work situation bleed all over the rest of his life, whereas Marisela puts the misfortune of losing her job neatly into a box and goes about the rest of her life as normally as possible. Marcos's explanatory style is universal, whereas Marisela's is specific.

The reason these first two dimensions are so important for realistic optimism is that they affect helplessness directly: When we find temporary causes for our troubles, we limit helplessness in time; and when we find specific causes for our troubles, we limit helplessness to its original situation. When we control helplessness through this mindset, we develop a very powerful feeling that allows us to overcome most of the bad events—the feeling of hope.

The last dimension of our explanatory style relates to how we assign blame after bad things happen. If we *personalize* the failure or setback, we tend to blame ourselves for what happened and may believe that we are worthless and talentless. However, if we externalize the blame, we look for external circumstances to explain what happened. We maintain our self-esteem and continue to feel okay about ourselves.

Marcos was convinced that the reason he lost his job was his poor performance. Marisela, on the other hand, repeatedly told herself, "This is due to corporate cost-cutting and has nothing to do with my performance." That made the whole difference to how they thought about themselves in relation to the setback.

In short, permanence controls how long we suffer, pervasiveness controls which situations we are suffering in, and personalization controls how we feel about ourselves. So how does all of this relate to assuming positive intentions?

Seligman's explanatory styles relate mainly to dealing with negative events, but we can apply the principles to dealing with others. The main dimension of assuming positive intention is being realistically optimistic about people (and their intentions). Let's say you're working with a colleague on an important project. Just before you submit the final report, you notice they have made a significant mistake in the financial analyses. If you assume the worst, you may think they are going to make similar mistakes in the future (permanence: this is going to continue to happen). And since they made a financial mistake, chances are they also make writing mistakes and their work is probably based on wrong assumptions (pervasiveness: they are bad at everything). And finally, you are likely to think that the mistake was due to their incompetence, laziness, or negligence (personalization: it is 100 percent their fault).

However, if you switch your thinking and assume positive intentions, you may think: They made this one mistake, but they are going to learn and will not make this type of mistake again (short term). Also, they made a finance mistake, but I know they are good at other things (specific). And it is possible that they were working late because of the deadline and have too much on their plate because we are short-staffed. So the mistake is likely not due to their skills but rather the situation they found themselves in (impersonal).

This is a much more functional way of thinking about that person if we want to continue to work with them and trust them in the future, and it's also much less frustrating. And at the same time, it still allows for accountability and reassessment. If the colleague makes a similar mistake next week, makes other types of mistakes in the future, or proves to be incompetent or lazy, we will stop extending these generous interpretations to them.

AS WE'VE SEEN, it's not everyone's default setting to apply optimism to bad situations or negative behaviors. But we can actually learn how do it—that's why Seligman talks about *learned optimism*. How do we learn it? Let's start by looking at the three stages that we typically go through when we are interpreting negative events: adversity, belief, and consequences.

Let's say you are busy at work on a day packed with meetings and crises. As you're rushing from one meeting to another, your spouse calls you. This creates a (minor) form of *adversity*: Now you have to deal with this call, on top of everything else you're dealing with. Immediately, a negative *belief* may start forming: "Why are they calling me now and wasting my time? Don't they realize how busy I am?" The *consequence* is you may answer the phone curtly: "What do you need? I am very busy right now!" Your spouse feels bad about calling you and quickly ends the call. The interaction is likely to create tension when you go home that evening.

It is possible to change the situation if we challenge the action by introducing *disputation*. After the tense phone call, if you have a few minutes to yourself later on that day, you can intentionally dispute your beliefs and tell yourself: "Don't be so hard on them. They didn't realize that the call would distract me. They probably thought it would be a nice break. It's sweet that they think about me when we're apart. I'm glad I have such a kind and supportive spouse." This reframing is likely to make you more relaxed and feel better about your spouse and your relationship. You may call them back, explain why you were curt, and apologize.

How can we learn how to dispute our beliefs? These four mindset shifts are needed:

1. Evidence
2. Alternatives
3. Implications
4. Usefulness

Consider this workplace scenario. You worked hard on a report for your boss and emailed it to her before you left in the evening. The following morning, you see your boss in the hallway. You approach her to say hello, but she frowns at you. You immediately think to yourself, "The report is very bad. I'm going to get fired." You start feeling helpless and spend the whole morning catastrophizing.

When something like this happens to us, disputation is the key to overcoming our dark mood: We need to dispute our pessimistic explanations and replace them with optimistic ones. The first mindset shift is to look for the *evidence*: "What is the evidence for and against my beliefs that my report is bad, it made the boss frown, and I am going to get fired?" We can ask ourselves the following questions:

- On what grounds did I think it was my report that made my boss frown?
- Do I know of anything wrong with my report?
- Did I consider all the important factors?
- Are my conclusions based on the facts in front of me?
- Has my boss even read the report yet, or is it still unread in her inbox?

When we go into detective mode and question our assumptions in this way, we will often find we have jumped to the worst possible conclusion without any solid evidence.

The second mindset shift is to look for *alternatives*—other ways to interpret the adversity. You might consider different explanations along these lines:

- Could it be that my boss is worried about something related to her family?

- Is it possible that my boss got stuck in some bad traffic this morning? Or maybe she hasn't had the chance to get her morning coffee?

- Could she be frowning because she is expecting a difficult phone call with her own boss?

If our automatically pessimistic interpretations have gone unchallenged for years and become ingrained in our thinking, the alternative explanations may not come to us easily. That's why it is important to intentionally take the time to think up these possible alternatives.

The third mindset shift is to think about what the possible *implications* of our pessimistic assumptions would be if they were accurate:

- What is the worst thing that can happen? Is it the end of the world?

- What is the evidence that this boss fires people for bad reports?

- Am I really going to get fired for one slipup?

These questions can help us to de-catastrophize the situation by confronting the most realistic implications.

The final mindset shift is to think about the *usefulness* of ruminating about what happened. "How does it help me now to think all morning about my boss's frown? Wouldn't it be better for me if I actually do my other work while waiting for the boss to talk to me?" Sometimes the accuracy of our explanations is not what really matters.

What matters is whether spending time on the problem now will do any good.

Let's apply these mindset shifts to a real-life situation: a first-time manager working with a colleague. Jim, a young healthcare leader, was working on a large project to expand a service line and proposed hiring additional clinicians. Shana was the new financial analyst in charge of reviewing requests before they go to the CEO.

Jim started hearing from others that Shana was against the project. On his way home one day, a team member called him and told him that Shana had removed the request for the additional clinicians from the proposal. Jim became upset. Why was Shana sabotaging his plan? At home, he spent the whole evening going through negative explanations for Shana's behaviors: "She must have some hidden agenda. She only cares about herself. She doesn't respect me." He barely got any sleep all night.

The following morning, Jim sped to the office to prepare for battle. As soon as Shana arrived, he stormed into her office, all guns blazing. He accused her of sabotaging his plan and called her selfish and inconsiderate. His tirade went on for several minutes. Shana sat there in stunned silence.

How could Jim have applied the realistic optimism mindset to deal differently with the situation? Let's go back to adversity, belief, and consequences. As soon as Jim heard about Shana's action to remove the request, he felt the *adversity*. That in turn resulted in his *belief* that Shana was acting maliciously. The *consequence* was for him to barge into her office and confront her.

What if Jim had taken a moment that evening to challenge his beliefs about Shana's actions? He could have applied the four shifts of disputation:

1. Evidence: What evidence do I have that Shana is acting maliciously and wants to sabotage my plan? What do I know about Shana's character? Have I seen her sabotage other projects in the past?

2. Alternatives: What are possible explanations for what Shana did? What could her motive be? Does Shana know something I don't? Is it possible that the rumors are not true?

3. Implications: So what if Shana has removed the request? Is this the end of the world? Can I still salvage the request by talking to the CEO directly? Do I want to ruin my relationship with Shana because of one incident?

4. Usefulness: How helpful is it for me to spend my whole evening thinking about this without having additional information? Could I focus on something else and leave this till the morning?

If Jim had applied these disputation skills, he would likely have withheld judgment and waited for the morning to talk to Shana. He would have respectfully asked whether she removed the request and why.

What actually happened is that when Jim finally stopped yelling, Shana quietly explained that she had temporarily removed the request from the proposal because she thought she should have a conversation with the CEO first to justify the additional spending. If the CEO saw the proposal with the original request for more providers, she reasoned, he may reject the project on the spot. Jim was shocked. Shana did not sabotage his plan—she had likely saved it.

Realistic optimism is about intentionally pausing to assess and dispute our negative assumptions towards others. In the next chapter, we will learn another mindset shift: empathy and humanizing others.

— 7 —

Empathy

AT THE peak of the COVID pandemic, Dave Jeppesen held a town-hall-style call every week with his boss, the governor of Idaho. As the state health director, Dave updated the public on prevention guidelines and case numbers. More than 100,000 people attended each call. Many of the people attending were not well-informed on the science of pandemics, and when given the chance to ask questions, they had some very strong opinions. Dave recalls, "We had a lot of interesting people on the call. Some of them were victims of disinformation or had strong beliefs in conspiracies."

It would have been very easy for Dave to look down on them and answer their questions condescendingly. But he adopted a different approach: "I tried to go into every call with the mindset of openness, curiosity, and empathy," he told me. "I had to remind myself that the other person is a human who is afraid and worried about their loved ones, so who am I to judge them?"

While it was very hard to do in the moment, Dave continued to empathize with everyone on the call. He recalled an 88-year-old man who attended every call and asked a lot of questions, many stemming from conspiracy theories. It was very tempting for Dave to dismiss him or even make fun of his opinions. But he knew that behind his opinions, the man was just afraid. "So, I tried to connect to him. Instead of saying 'You're crazy, don't take horse tranquilizers!' I would say to him, 'I understand your concern, let me tell you what I know and why.' If I had responded in a dismissive way, then the other 99,999 people would have tuned me out."

WHAT WE can learn from Dave is that to assume positive intentions towards others, it helps to humanize them. And to humanize requires a significant mindset shift: Even if they are saying things that don't make sense to us or behaving negatively towards us, we need to think of them as flesh-and-blood human beings with concerns and fears. This requires us to get past our own fears and switch our brain from an emotional state to a rational state. It is well established that the human brain, put very simply, consists of an emotional limbic system and a rational cortex system. To humanize, we need to activate the latter and deactivate the former. And when we overcome our fears, we can help others overcome theirs as well.

But humanizing others does not seem to be our default system. We dehumanize because we are inclined to think in terms of "us vs. them." We perceive the world in a tribal way: I belong to the tribe of logical, well-informed, good people, and those belonging to other tribes are the opposite. Tribal thinking can apply to all aspects of our lives. In my professional life, my tribe is my department and colleagues. In politics, it is my party and political leaders. In religion, it's the people who share my beliefs and practices. And so on. Of course, we need these tribes to belong to and to thrive. But the danger is when we think of our groups as always good and right and of the others as always bad and wrong. If we were to check honestly, we would catch ourselves frequently dehumanizing people who belong to other tribes.

For example, I am a fan of Manchester United, a famous football club in England (that is real football, which Americans insist on calling "soccer"). I have been supporting United since 1990, and when I think of other United fans, I think of them as passionate, well-informed, loyal people, just like me. Now, it happens that Manchester United and Liverpool FC have one of the fiercest historical rivalries in football. And when I think of Liverpool fans, I think of them as irritating, fickle, and violent. Without even realizing it, I dehumanize them.

The research shows I am not alone. In one study, researchers brought a group of Manchester United fans to a university campus and had them answer questions that reminded them of how much they loved their team. The fans were then asked to move to a different room, and on their way they encountered a person wearing a football jersey and appearing to be injured and in need of help. What the fans didn't know was that the "injured fan" was a research accomplice. When the accomplice was wearing a United jersey, 92 percent of the United fans stopped to help him, but when it was a Liverpool jersey, only 30 percent of the United fans stopped to help. Even when they saw an injured person in clear need of assistance, they dehumanized him because they saw him as belonging to the enemy tribe.

The researchers then changed the experiment slightly and brought in another group of very similar United fans. This time they asked them questions that made them think of how much they loved football as a sport. The rest of the experiment was exactly the same, and the number of United fans stopping to help the "injured" accomplice was similar to that in the first experiment. However, when the accomplice was wearing a Liverpool jersey, the proportion of United fans who stopped to help jumped from 30 percent to 70. The questions that reminded them of what they loved about football caused them to think of themselves as part of the tribe of football-loving fans, not just United fans.

When we think about how different members of other tribes are, we assume negative intention and don't want to deal with them. However, when we are reminded of what brings us together and what is common between us, we may assume positive intention and extend a helping hand. The problem is that real life usually does not, on its own, give us reminders about how similar we are. So we have to remind ourselves.

One thought experiment I force myself to do every time I am watching a football game and see images of rival fans screaming for their teams is to try to think of them as human beings: "This person was probably born in

Liverpool and his father was a Liverpool fan that used to take him to games as a boy. He grew up loving his hometown team, and now he takes his own kids to watch every Sunday. He may have issues at work or personal problems, but when Liverpool does well, he is happy. In fact, we are very similar!" This thought exercise does not diminish my loyalty to my team or my banter with rival fans. But it takes the edge off my tribalism. And it helps me sleep better at night when United loses (which unfortunately happens a lot these days).

The same thought process can apply where sports and national pride come together. Organizational psychologist Adam Grant has studied the difference between positive patriotism and negative patriotism within the context of the Olympic Games. He argues that positive patriotism is about loving and supporting your country while still cheering on or at least respecting athletes from other countries. Negative patriotism is about looking down on other countries. I confess to engaging in a lot of negative patriotism over the years, but more recently, while working on this book, I have committed to the more positive version. (For example, I am not crazy about the Australian swimmers competing against Americans at the Olympics, but I can appreciate their athleticism and love for their country.)

YOU MAY BE THINKING, "Sure, applying humanization to sports is fine, but can we practice it in more serious or sensitive situations?" My colleague Donovan, whom you met in chapter 1, told me about a time he was at a grocery store on Halloween night. As he was grabbing snacks for a party, he noticed another shopper whose face was painted black. (You may remember that Donovan is African American.) Donovan was shocked. How can someone in this day and age still do this? Other shoppers also noticed and were sending disapproving looks at black-face guy. In the parking lot, Donovan saw the same man heading towards his car. Despite how upset he felt about it, Donovan forced himself to think: "Why would a decent person paint his face black? There must be a reason." He decided to talk to him. Donovan put on his best smile and approached him in a friendly way: "Hey man, are you going to a Halloween party tonight?"

Black-face guy was surprised, and then he realized what Donovan meant. Embarrassed, he admitted, "Hey man, I know how this looks—everyone was about to kill me inside! But I swear I am not doing blackface. I am not that kind of person." Then he reached inside his car and revealed the rest of his costume: He was supposed to be a black skeleton with a scary mask, but the mask didn't cover all his face, so he painted it all black to cover up the parts that were showing. He explained that when he got in his car, he took the mask off and then forgot to put it back on before he went into the store.

"I try to do this with everyone. I try to see their humanity, even if they do something that upsets me," Donovan said. "It doesn't mean I accept racism; I just try to give people the benefit of the doubt and check with them first."

Again, I don't share this example to suggest we need to give racists the benefit of the doubt. Of course not. I share it because sometimes there may be another explanation. And, when appropriate, it's a good practice to assume provisionally that there is and to check with the other person.

Simran Jeet Singh, the educator and practicing Sikh we met in chapter 5, tried to apply humanizing others to an even more difficult situation. In 2012, a mass shooter walked into a Sikh temple in Milwaukee and killed six innocent people while they were praying. After months of mourning and grief, Simran was desperate for something to help him move on from the tragedy.

He tried to force himself to feel compassion and love towards the shooter. But no matter how hard he tried, he just couldn't feel anything other than rage. There was no way he was going to forgive him. He tried to humanize the shooter, to find similarities with him, but he couldn't find any: The shooter was very different in his values and behavior. Then it occurred to Simran that ignoring the differences was not the way to go. He realized he needed to acknowledge the differences and look for the shooter's deeper humanity. Yes, he had lived a very different life and committed a heinous crime, but he still had the same human light inside him. By focusing on the common humanity, Simran was able to accept the situation, even if he did not forgive the shooter. (I'll discuss forgiveness more in chapter 10.) Again, this has nothing to do with the shooter and everything to do with Simran himself and how he chose to cope with the situation to reduce his own suffering.

At the heart of humanizing others is feeling empathy towards them. To feel empathy after someone does something questionable or makes a mistake, we need to put ourselves in their shoes, assume that they are a basically reasonable person, and ask, "Why would a reasonable person act like this? There must be an explanation."

Moreover, we could ask the question that sociologist Brené Brown encourages us to ask: "What if the other person is trying their best?" Let's say you send an email to a colleague requesting some information and they don't answer till the following day. Instead of getting annoyed with them and assuming they don't care, what if you reminded yourself of how busy they are? Research has shown that any typical person has at least 150 different tasks on their plate at a given time, and that an executive's to-do list for a single day could take more than a week to finish. If we remind ourselves of that, we may give our colleague the benefit of the doubt because we assume they are trying their best.

In her leadership workshops, Brown asks participants to think of someone who makes them feel frustrated, disappointed, or resentful. She then asks them to consider the possibility that this other person might be trying their best. This shift in mindset can help us feel empathy towards them. Instead of continuing to harass them, for example, we may choose to start helping them. Instead of sending another message and hurrying them to reply to our email ("Per my message below from yesterday, I am still waiting for your response"), we could offer to help them with some of their tasks. This doesn't mean we don't hold others accountable when their behavior is repeatedly unprofessional; it just means that when appropriate, we put ourselves in their shoes.

Brown defines empathy as "taking the perspective of another person, becoming the listener and the student, not the knower/teacher." This requires us to stay away from judgment and attempt to understand what emotions they might be experiencing. Please note that trying to understand what they are going through and feeling does not mean that we take on these feelings. Empathic concern, which is what we are advocating for here, involves wanting to understand and help the other person. This is very different and generally more productive than emotional empathy, which involves totally taking on someone else's feelings.

Another approach to practicing empathy and humanizing others after they do something wrong is to force ourselves to answer a very tough question: "Have I done something similar to this in the past?" This question enables us to be honest with ourselves. And most of the time, we will realize that we have indeed done something similar. Which doesn't make it okay—it just makes us feel more similar to them and empathetic towards them.

I tried experimenting with this approach over a two-week period. Every time I got annoyed by the actions of a colleague, friend, family member, or total stranger, I asked myself if I had done something similar in the past. Here are the results:

- "Have I ever stood at the very front of the A line while boarding a Southwest flight even though my boarding pass clearly said A5?" Yes!

- "Have I ever turned right on a red light even though the sign clearly said No Right Turn on Red?" Yes!
- "Have I ever left a dirty dish in the sink despite the dishwasher being empty?" Yes!
- "Have I ever left a text message unanswered for a whole day even though I could have answered it earlier?" Yes!

Since I have done all of these things myself (some of them repeatedly and intentionally), what right do I have to judge others when they engage in exactly the same behaviors? We all want others to show grace when we mess up, so why do we not do the same when the roles are reversed?

There are some parallel examples that organization leaders can ask themselves. Here are a few:

- "Have I ever arrived late to a meeting because I left home late without a valid excuse?"
- "Have I ever rolled my eyes at a colleague's suggestion because it didn't fit with my plan?"
- "Have I ever not given a team member any attention when I passed them in the hallway because I was preoccupied with my next meeting?"
- "Have I ever accidentally or intentionally hit Reply All on an email that could have just gone to one person?"

———

OF ALL THE EXAMPLES of empathy and humanization, perhaps the most unlikely and most significant is that of President John F. Kennedy during the Cuban Missile Crisis. On the morning of October 16, 1962, the CIA woke up Kennedy with the news that the Soviet Union had constructed medium- and long-range ballistic nuclear missile sites in Cuba, just 90 miles from American shores. The threat of a nuclear war that might destroy the whole world was as real as it has ever been.

Most of Kennedy's advisors recommended an immediate and aggressive response: the US using all of its military might to destroy the sites. There was no time to waste and attack was the only option, they argued. But Kennedy pushed back. He urged everyone to calm down and think clearly about the issue from different perspectives.

A few years before, Kennedy had read a book on nuclear strategy, and one of the passages from the book had caught his attention. The author advised that in a nuclear crisis, "Keep strong, if possible. In any case, keep cool. Have unlimited patience. Never corner an opponent, and always assist him to save face. Put yourself in his shoes—so as to see things through his eyes."

When the missile crisis began, Kennedy remembered the book and started asking his advisors, "Why are the Soviets doing this? What advantage are they seeking? They must have a reason!" This mindset allowed the president and his cabinet to start to imagine what the world looked like to the Soviets. The more they put themselves in their adversary's shoes, the more they realized how threatening the world looked to them. Kennedy's counterpart, Nikita Khrushchev, was hiding under his tough-guy persona to cover up his fears and insecurities. Only someone in a desperate position would take such an enormous risk, Kennedy argued.

These discussions provided the president with new insights: Striking the missile bases would be the most irrevocable option with the highest risk. It would leave the Soviets with no choice but to strike back on American cities to protect their own soldiers and save face. So instead of a military option, Kennedy discussed a blockade of Cuba. While it was not a popular option among his advisors, he liked this approach because it would give him and the Soviets more options. It afforded both parties the chance to evaluate their choices with calm and logical thinking.

Once the Americans announced the blockade, Khrushchev had time to think. He finally wrote to Kennedy comparing the situation they were in to that of pulling a rope with a knot in it from two opposite directions. The knot was representative of the all-out war. The harder they pulled, he explained, the less likely it was they would ever be able to untie the knot. The Soviets communicated that they were open to negotiating the removal of the missiles if the US offered a few compromises. And just like that, cool heads prevailed and the crisis was over. It's not an exaggeration to say that I wouldn't be writing this book, and you wouldn't be reading it, if Kennedy had chosen the war alternative.

Empathy and humanization saved the world from nuclear apocalypse. And they can help leaders improve relations and get better outcomes. Whether you are negotiating a major deal with a rival company or agreeing on a new plan with your team members, it is always valuable to assume positive intent and empathize with others. In the next chapter, we will build on these ideas and explore another mindset shift necessary for assuming positive intentions: humility, awareness, and open-mindedness.

— 8 —

Humility

ONE OF THE MOST INFLUENTIAL commencement speeches, in my opinion, is the one that David Foster Wallace gave at Kenyon College in 2005. It is titled "This Is Water," and in the opening passage, Wallace tells the story of two young fish swimming along. The two fish encounter an older fish swimming in the other direction. The older fish greets them: "Morning, boys. How's the water?" The two young fish continue swimming, and then one of them looks over at the other and goes, "What the hell is water?"

Wallace's premise is that like the young fish, we all become so stuck in our own ways of thinking that we stop seeing what is around us, and things become hidden in plain sight. Rather than considering other people's motivations, urges, and feelings, we only think about our own. Wallace explains, "Everything in my own immediate experience supports my deep belief that I am the absolute center of the universe; the realest, most vivid and important person in existence. [...] It is our default setting, hard-wired into our boards at birth."

This natural default setting of being "uniquely, completely alone in our heads" every single moment of every day leads to a sort of arrogance that is based on blind certainty: We think we know everything based on our own perceptions and interpretations of other people's behaviors. This closed-mindedness "amounts to an imprisonment so total that the prisoner doesn't even know he's locked up," Wallace explains. We are all prisoners in our own heads.

So how do we change the default setting and free ourselves? It is not about learning how to think, Wallace argues. It is about choosing what to think *about*. It is about being aware enough to choose what we pay attention to and how we construct meaning from our experiences.

As an example, Wallace presents a situation that adults experience on a regular basis. After a long day at work, we drive home in horrible traffic. But we've got no food at home, so we are forced to stop at a grocery store crowded with other adults who are going through similar days. Our default reaction is to think of every car on the road, and every person at the store, as another obstacle we have to get around. "This is really all about me—*my* hungriness and *my* fatigue and *my* desire to just get home, and everybody else is just in my way." When we are in our default setting, the cars on the road seem large and ugly and driven by insensitive jerks, and the people in the grocery store appear rude and loud and annoying.

This type of thinking is automatic, natural, and self-centered, and it happens to all of us. But we can choose to think differently. We can change the default setting and get out of our own heads. Wallace encourages us to make this shift by rejecting blind certainty and practicing open-mindedness and humility.

Humility and open-mindedness can change our perspective on the people at the grocery store, he explains. "You can choose to look differently at this fat, dead-eyed, over-made-up lady who just screamed at her kid in the checkout line. Maybe she's not usually like this. Maybe she's been up three straight nights holding the hand of a husband who is dying of bone cancer. Or maybe this very lady is the low-wage clerk at the motor vehicle department, who just yesterday helped your spouse resolve a horrific, infuriating red-tape problem through some small act of bureaucratic kindness." This change in our default setting requires us to turn our attention from ourselves to others in a humble and open-minded way. (I have written about humility and open-mindedness in depth in my previous book, *Humbitious*.) That, in turn, will help us assume positive intentions in the other shoppers, drivers, and everyone else.

THE WORD *humility* comes from the Latin root *humus*, which means "ground" or "earth." To adopt a humble mindset, we need to get out of our own head and be close to the ground, close to other people. This requires us to question our view of reality and to be open-minded to other possibilities.

The default setting of thinking of everyone as an obstacle or threat is a type of self-protective strategy. If we prepare ourselves for a bad event, it can't hurt us anymore.

We do it to avoid being caught by surprise and to be safe. In her insightful TED Talk, executive and performance coach Lynn Carnes tells an illustrative story.

One day, Lynn got to the airport a bit late for her flight. In the TSA PreCheck line in front of her was a lady with a baby and multiple bags. Lynn's first reaction was "Why does this need to be in front of me now? And why does she even have pre-check? Isn't this line supposed to be for busy professionals like me?" (I admit I have had these same thoughts myself.) The line was barely advancing, and Lynn became more and more irritated.

Once the lady finally got to the TSA screening checkpoint, she had trouble getting her ID out of her purse and managing her bags, so she had to put her baby on the floor. In that instant, Lynn saw a human being struggling to get through a checkpoint with a baby to take care of. She didn't see an obstacle anymore. Lynn immediately reached out to help the lady with her bags. Her whole demeanor changed, and she was more relaxed. The situation was still the same, but she had chosen to think about it differently.

How do we set ourselves up to change our thinking like Lynn did, even when unprompted by a baby lying on the airport floor? I have found that it's important to give ourselves more time and become less rushed. When time is scarce, as it typically is, we tend to stay in our default setting.

For example, if I have somewhere to be, such as a class to teach or a doctor's appointment, I intentionally leave 15 minutes before the time I actually need to. Also, I travel regularly for work and try to get to the airport an hour and a half before my flight. Many people would think that is not an efficient use of time, but I do it for a specific purpose: I don't want to be so pressed for time that I start seeing people and cars around me as hurdles in my way. I want to have the luxury to get out of their way and be kind and considerate to them. I want to yield to the other car on the highway. If I see someone rushing behind me in the TSA line, I want to offer them my spot. I don't have to leave early, but I choose to so that I can perceive the world around me differently. It is much better for my own mental health and happiness because I arrive at my destination more relaxed and tend be a more pleasant human being.

This type of thinking requires humility. And at the center of humility is open-mindedness, which doesn't just apply to situations with strangers on the highway or in airports. It also applies to conversations with people we already know, such as colleagues at work. "The test of open-mindedness is ... whether or not we are prepared to entertain doubts about our views," explains philosophy professor William Hare of Dalhousie University. Open-mindedness is an attitude towards our beliefs that consists of a genuine readiness to revise them when called for. It does not mean a lack of commitment to a certain view; it just means a willingness to subject our view to further review and scrutiny.

When Benjamin Franklin decided to become more humble and open-minded, he started to become more intentional about the words he used in conversation. As he described it, "I forbid myself [...] the use of every word or expression in the language that imported a fixed opinion, such as *certainly*, *undoubtedly*, etc., and I adopted, instead of them, I *conceive*, I *apprehend*, or I *imagine* a thing to be so or so, or it so *appears* to me *at present*." Franklin aimed to start his sentences with "I could be wrong, but..." in order to prime himself to be open-minded about changing his opinion.

Open-mindedness starts with curiosity about others and their feelings, motivations, and intentions. When examining curiosity in the context of human interactions, it is important to remember the origin of the word itself. *Curiosity* comes from the Latin *cura*, which means *care* or *concern*. This implies that we can't be curious about someone unless we care about them.

A natural byproduct of curiosity is asking good questions that are genuine attempts to learn. Former MIT organizational development professor Edgar Schein referred to this approach as "humble inquiry." He described it as "the fine art of drawing someone out, of asking questions to which you don't already have the answer, of building a relationship based on curiosity and interest in the other person."

Can we apply open-mindedness and curiosity to situations where others appear to be acting negatively towards us? Lynn Carnes thinks so. She shares an example from an off-site meeting she facilitated for a corporate team. Lynn had been working with the team for a while and had done several off-sites with them. That morning, one of the leaders on the team, Joe, appeared to be irritated. Once Lynn started explaining the plan for the session, he raised his hand and asked, "Can we just do something different?"

Lynn's immediate reaction was to be shocked and irritated by the comment. In that moment, she was tempted to respond negatively to his comment and fight back. She could have stayed in her default setting—seeing Joe as an obstacle to having a productive session.

But instead she was mindful enough to pause a bit before she responded. She decided to be open-minded and curious. So she asked Joe and the rest of the team, "Yes, what is it going to take for this team to have different conversations?" Instead of seeing him as the antagonistic person, she saw him as the caring teammate. Her question and reframing allowed Joe to reengage, and he actually became the most enthusiastic member of the team that day. Even though Joe started negatively, Lynn's humble and open-minded question opened the door for him to change his attitude.

It helps to remember that, just like Lynn, we almost always have a choice. We don't have to react right away; we can pause and assume positive intent. When we pause, we allow ourselves to think of a different story in which the other person is not a villain and we are not a victim. We see a small sliver of positivity in them, and that will likely nudge them to act that way.

THE KEY TO approaching people and situations with humility and open-mindedness is learning how to overcome our confirmation bias. Confirmation bias is our tendency to form opinions based on previous experiences and interpret all future events based on those views. To overcome that, we need to proactively seek information that challenges our beliefs. We need to open our minds to other possible interpretations (more on that in the next chapter). The goal of this exercise (which is very similar to the disputation skill that we discussed before) is the disruption of our assumptions. We must attempt to interpret the situation from a new point of view and detach ourselves, even slightly, from the confirmation bias that led us to think about it in a negative way. This will allow us to be more open-minded about others' decisions and actions and to approach them with humility and curiosity.

One way to deal with confirmation bias is to break down situations into two components: our *beliefs* and the other person's *opinion*. Let's take this example: My boss did not include me on a new project, and I started thinking to myself, "She definitely feels threatened by me. She is so old-school and top-down. She wants to maintain power."

First, let's focus on the *belief* that my boss feels threatened by me and likes control. Where did this belief come from? There must be something in my past that led to it. What else has influenced my perception of my boss? Is it related to my experience working with a lot of companies that were top-down? Or to the previous bosses that never had my back? Maybe it's related to this boss and the times she dismissed my opinions in the past. It could be one thing or everything. The key is to recognize that this is the filter through which I am interpreting the situation.

Second, let's turn our attention to the other person's *opinion*. In this case, why does my boss not want me on the new project? The first interpretation that came to my mind is that she is threatened by me. But what are some others? If I use my imagination, I can think of quite a few, even if some of them are far-fetched. For example, maybe she wanted me on the project but couldn't add me because her superiors insisted on someone else. Or she is waiting to put me on a better project where I can really use my strengths.

The goal is not to be naïve or imagine things that don't exist. It is to try to think of alternative points of view and disconnect, even for a brief time, from confirmation biases. By doing this, I can then ask my boss directly: "Can you please explain why you didn't consider me for this project?"

My colleague Dave Jeppesen told me about a time when his company was negotiating with a big client. One of the team's salespeople was leading the negotiation and took it upon himself to offer the client a significant concession without checking with upper management. When the executives met to discuss the decision, many of them did not want to honor the offer. They were very upset with the salesperson, and some even wanted him fired. But then one executive asked, "What are the possible reasons that the salesperson offered the concession?"

The other executives were taken aback by the question; they hadn't even thought about the salesperson and his opinion. Their resistance was a product of previous experiences dealing with salespeople who perhaps were not competent or tended to be individualistic. They assumed that he offered the concession because he was negligent and didn't want to negotiate hard. But the question allowed everyone to pause and consider their confirmation biases. This created an opening: "Since we are not 100 percent certain why he did it, let's ask him."

They invited the salesperson to defend his action. He explained that the client had threatened to leave. The only way to save the relationship was to offer him the concession. The salesperson was not bad or selfish—he was resourceful. He had saved the relationship and with it had saved millions of dollars for the company.

Confirmation bias is especially problematic when we are in a position of authority and have more knowledge than other people. Clinical psychologist Dr. Daniel Lobel experienced that when he was starting his practice years ago. At the time, Dr. Lobel had contracted with the Department of Social Services to do yearly intellectual assessments for people receiving disability benefits because their brain function was impaired. The goal of the assessments was to make sure that the disability still existed and that the patient was entitled to receive the benefits.

One day, a young female patient came to Dr. Lobel's office with her mom. The patient was disabled due to fetal alcohol syndrome, which is caused by the mother ingesting significant amounts of alcohol during gestation. This can cause irreversible brain damage in the child, leading to very low IQ and struggles with basic life functions.

In addition to her cognitive disability, this specific young patient also suffered from distorted facial features and problems with her hands and fingers, all due to fetal alcohol syndrome. Despite her difficulties, she carried herself with unusual grace, and she proudly shared with Dr. Lobel that she was so happy to be working as a bagger at a grocery store. Dr. Lobel was moved deeply by her attitude. At the same time, he felt an overwhelming sense of anger towards the mother who so carelessly inflicted all this pain on this wonderful young woman.

Towards the end of the visit, Dr. Lobel asked to speak to the mom, who had been sitting in the waiting room. Here is how their conversation went:

> DR. L.: Your daughter was very pleasant and cooperative during the examination.
>
> MOM: She always tries to do her best.
>
> DR. L.: I can see that. But she will always need to be cared for.
>
> MOM: Yes, we know that. We have made appropriations for her after we are gone.
>
> DR. L.: That is a tremendous responsibility you have.
>
> MOM: I know. We weren't planning on keeping her.
>
> [Dr. Lobel looked at her quizzically.]
>
> MOM: We took her as a temporary emergency foster care placement, but we fell in love with her and adopted her.

Dr. Lobel was shocked. He had judged the mother as an uncaring and neglectful parent, whereas in fact she was one of the most caring parents he had ever met. He thought she was the one who had ruined her child's life, but actually she had saved it. His blind certainty and confirmation bias predisposed him to think about the mother in that way. That lesson taught him to be humble and open-minded, and stayed with him for the rest of his career. "I've found that the benefits of greater humility are extensive, personally and professionally. It gives me a greater open-mindedness. A constant awareness that there is always more to situations than we can see, and an openness to finding new information."

Epictetus, the stoic philosopher, argued that every event has two handles. We decide which handle we'll use to "carry" it afterwards. He said, "If your brother acts unjustly, do not lay hold of the act by that handle wherein he acts unjustly, for this is the handle which cannot be borne: but lay hold of the other, that he is your brother, that he was nurtured with you, and you will lay hold of the thing by that handle by which it can be borne." This understanding of the two handles requires open-mindedness. And likewise, if someone who reports to you has made a bad error of judgment, your immediate instinct may be to focus on that and direct everything you say to criticism and correction of it. But the stronger handle for you to hold on to will be the positive relationship between the two of you and the shared dedication to the company's goals. That handle can carry the weight of the correction.

In the next chapter, we will build on this idea and explore the importance of reality testing.

— 9 —

Reality Testing

ESTHER, AN EXECUTIVE in a large healthcare organization, had never experienced something like this before. One of her managers had just called to tell her that an employee in the marketing department had asked to work from home the day before. However, when the manager checked the electronic log-in records at the end of the day, they found that the employee did not log in to her company laptop even once all day. The manager felt the employee had betrayed his trust and lied to him about how she would spend her day. For him, this was a clear case of an employee pretending to do work while enjoying a day off on the company's dime. It was serious enough to be cause for immediate termination. The manager urged Esther to start a disciplinary process with human resources.

Esther listened intently and validated the manager's feelings. And then she paused for a moment to consider the situation. She had learned over the years not to jump to conclusions and to test reality from different perspectives. She asked the manager if he had talked to the employee in question to get her side of the story. The manager felt he didn't need to because it was obvious the employee had lied to him. He said he didn't trust anything she might tell him. Esther insisted and asked the manager to set up a three-way call with the employee right away.

Esther took the lead, starting the call by presenting the facts to the employee: "You asked to work from home yesterday, but there is no electronic evidence that you logged in to your laptop. We wanted to ask you what happened."

The employee was visibly upset. She replied, "I am so sorry for causing this situation, and I know how it looks—it looks like I lied. But what really happened is that I tried to log in to my laptop in the morning, but it wouldn't boot. It's an old laptop and I have been having trouble with it for a while. I called IT, but they said they couldn't help me because I wasn't connected to the company network. Since my plan for the day was to conduct market research on our competitors, I decided to use my daughter's computer. I swear that I worked my full shift, and I can show you the complete report with the results of my analyses."

Esther was relieved. The manager had jumped to a negative conclusion and almost started a chain of events to fire an innocent employee. His feelings of betrayal had clouded his judgment and prevented him from checking reality. Esther also realized that the organizational policy on working from home needed to be updated—it needed to clearly state that work can only be done using a company device.

After the call ended, Esther discussed the situation with the manager, and they decided to give the employee a verbal warning. She knew the employee could have made up the whole story; she may have spent the day watching TV or shopping, and the market analysis report was based on work she had done before. Therefore, she asked the manager to keep a close eye on her.

HOW DO leaders like Esther know they are not getting played? How much diligence is worthwhile? A basic level of trust is needed, while accepting the risk that others may not live up to that trust. But it is a risk worth taking, because otherwise companies would have to install security cameras in their employees' homes to make sure they are working when they say they are. That would be an extreme measure that would make trustworthy employees feel like children and is guaranteed to decrease autonomy and engagement. One equivalent to this risk-benefit analysis is the way retail stores think about theft: Retailers make conscious decisions about how much loss from customer theft is tolerable, in exchange for not making good customers feel mistrusted and not spending their whole budget on security.

Good leaders are realistically optimistic about others, empathetic towards them, and humble in their way of thinking. They trust and give the benefit of the doubt. And when someone appears to have done something wrong, they offer them the chance to explain themselves. They check the reality and do their due diligence, without paranoia or mistrust.

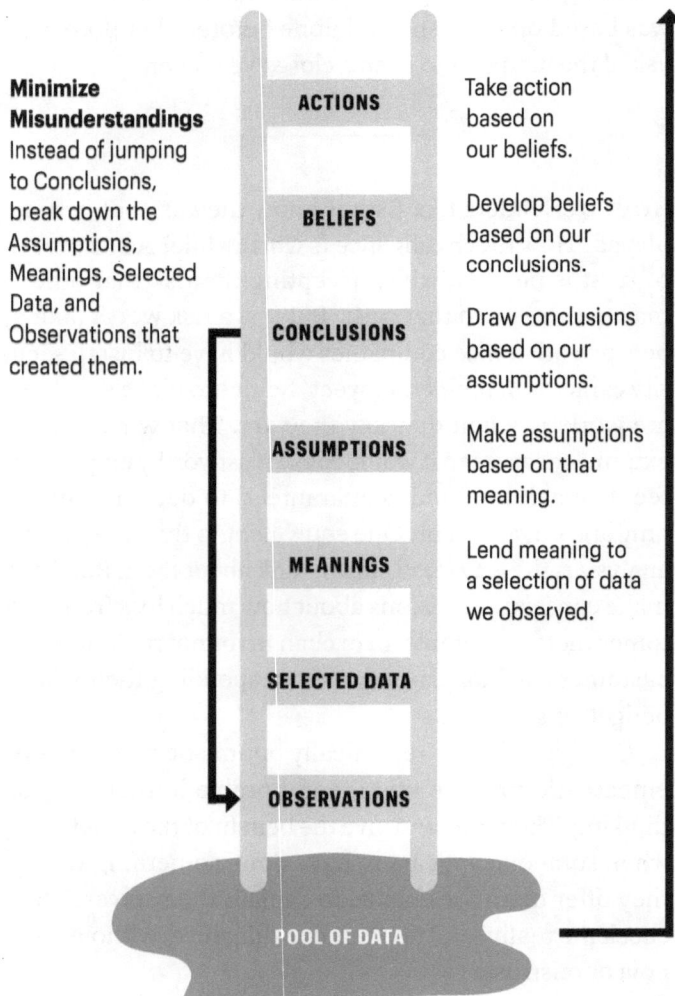

The three main steps in reality testing are:

1. Check yourself and your assumptions.
2. Check with others who are close to the situation.
3. Check with the main person in question.

For step 1, we should understand how we typically make assumptions in the first place:

1. We start by *observing* our past experiences.
2. We then *select* data from what we observe.
3. Then we add *meaning* to that data based on our personal and cultural backgrounds and biases.
4. Based on those meanings, we make *assumptions*.
5. These assumptions lead us to draw *conclusions* about people and situations.
6. Those conclusions predispose us to start adopting *beliefs* about the world.
7. These beliefs then dictate the *actions* we usually take.

This process is referred to as the "ladder of inference" and is generally a very efficient way to make quick decisions on busy days. However, when we leave our assumptions unchecked and untested, they can quickly lead to erroneous beliefs and unjustified negative actions.

Let me explain with a real example from my work as a professor. I was teaching a graduate class one day and noticed a student in the back row yawning. A few minutes into the session, he started to nod off. This annoyed me so much. The voice inside my head started telling me he is lazy and not interested in hearing the content that I had spent countless hours preparing. And then I remembered that this student was a bit of a jock. He had never taken class seriously; he just had this attitude about him like he didn't need to learn anything. He was probably out partying the night before. By the time I gave the class a short break, I had already decided: I was going to call him out in front of everyone to punish him for his lack of professionalism. He deserved it!

Now, let's step back and break down my thinking process using the seven-step assumption model:

1 I started with data that I *observed*: the student yawning and nodding off.

2 I then *selected* some details about his behavior: He is not paying any attention.

3 So I added some *meanings* of my own, based on my stereotypes about jocks: They don't care about academics, they are lazy and arrogant, etc.

4 I moved quickly up to making *assumptions* about him: He doesn't care.

5 And I *concluded* that he must have been partying late the night before.

6   I *believed* that he is not serious.

7   So what *action* is left for me other than to shame him publicly in front of the whole class?

As is clear in this example, the dangers of climbing the ladder of inference are significant. What I noticed about this student was influenced by my past experiences, assumptions, and beliefs. This is sometimes referred to as a "reflexive loop," but more generally psychologists call it confirmation bias (which we discussed in the last chapter). We all function according to self-generating assumptions and beliefs, and we are constantly looking for evidence that fits with them. With this focus, of course we find some evidence and therefore consider our beliefs verified, so we act on them without testing them.

But in this case, since I had been researching this topic for a while, another voice in my head said: *Stop. Don't call him out. Check your assumptions.* As we came back from the break, the student appeared to have freshened up a bit. He had a large cup of coffee and looked more engaged. Before the end of class, he even asked a good question.

As the class ended and everyone else left the room, I went to him and asked, "I noticed that you were a bit tired early on—what is going on?" He admitted with some embarrassment that he was indeed very tired. After a bit of hesitation, he shared that he works the early morning shift at a nearby department store to help pay his bills and tuition. My class starts at 9 a.m., and he had been at work from 4 a.m. until 8. Which meant that he had been awake since 3:30. Who wouldn't be tired with that schedule?

The way to avoid climbing up the ladder of inference every time we face a tricky situation is to take time to *reflect*. We need to become more aware of our own thinking by asking ourselves, "How did I come to this belief?" We also need to check the assumptions on which we are basing our conclusions. We need to interrogate ourselves: "What data did I base this assumption on? What am I missing?" And then we need to check the assumptions by asking the other person to explain their actions.

Think about what would have happened if I had actually called out the student in public. I would have felt good in the moment. His classmates would probably have enjoyed a good laugh at his expense. And it would probably have ruined our relationship forever. He would have started seeing me as the insensitive professor that humiliated him in public. We would both fly up our own ladders every time we interacted with each other: I would be looking for more evidence that he is lazy and unprofessional, and he'd be looking for more evidence that I am out to get him.

In these situations, just like with Esther's employee, certainly the other person may not tell the truth when we ask for their side of the story. My student could have been partying the night before, and the whole morning shift story was something he made up. All of that is possible. And unlikely. Most people are just trying their best. And that is why we have to check with them before jumping to conclusions. Because what is the alternative? Ask the student to show me his paystub? Get the phone number of his boss so I can verify his claims? That is not the way I choose to treat my students or anyone else.

Another important task in reality testing is to check with people who are familiar with the other person and with the situation. Before jumping to conclusions about a colleague's comment during a meeting, ask others who were there: "How did you perceive her comment? Why do you think she said what she said? What do you think she meant?" Often, other people who are not as emotionally invested in the situation as we are will inform us that we have misinterpreted the intentions of the other person.

SEEKING CLARIFICATIONS about the other person's intentions directly from them, and in a nonconfrontational style, is another powerful way to avoid stewing in our own emotions. That's how accountable positivity is created. When you treat people like trustworthy adults while also showing them you are not a naïve pushover, most will act like trustworthy adults and rarely betray your trust.

Accountable positivity is a helpful framework for dealing with mistakes. It starts with trusting team members and with the assumption that they are competent, intelligent, and trying their best. I learned this from Trinity University president Dr. Vanessa Beasley: When a team member makes a mistake, the first conversation is based on the premise that everyone makes mistakes and focuses on learning from the experience. The leader asks the employees about the reasons behind what happened and how they can be dealt with. If the team member makes the same mistake again, the second conversation then focuses on the barriers that got in the way of learning from the first mistake. The leader asks the person how they are planning to remove these barriers. If they make the same mistake a third time, however, it becomes clear that they have refused to learn from the previous instances. This then leads to specified consequences that start with a warning and may escalate all the way to termination.

Executive coach and author Melody Wilding shares some scripts we can use when seeking those clarifications. Here's how to API & Verify:

> "I felt a bit confused about your comment yesterday. I might have misunderstood, but it seemed like you had some concerns. Could you clarify your perspective?"
>
> "During our meeting, when you mentioned [specific topic], I interpreted it as [explain your perspective]. I wanted to make sure I understood your point correctly because I value your input."
>
> "I've noticed that when [situation] happens, I tell myself a story that [your interpretation or assumption]. I wanted to share this with you because I believe in open communication, and I'd like to understand your perspective better."

After we ask in this calm and intentional way, it is crucial for us to *listen to understand.* Very often we ask, but then we *listen to reply*. We begin to formulate our response as soon as the other person starts explaining. When we listen to reply, it is all about us. It is all about our ego and wanting to win the argument and defeat the other person. However, when we switch our mindset and listen to understand, it is all about the other person. We take ourselves out of the equation and put our ego on hold. We come into the conversation with humility and curiosity: "I may know a bit about what is going on, but I am open to the possibility that the other person will share a different truth."

Reality testing is a crucial component of emotional intelligence. Given the number of decisions we all make each day, it is important to make sure that they are based in reality. One of the best tools that executive coaches use to assess emotional intelligence with the leaders they work with is the EQ-i 2.0 assessment, which consists of five components—the one relevant to this discussion being the "decision-making" composite, which is made up of problem-solving, reality testing, and impulse control. Problem-solving involves effectively using our emotions to solve problems. Reality testing is related to seeing things for what they really are. And impulse control is about understanding the appropriate times and ways to act on emotions and impulses, and how to think before we act. All three components allow us to make better decisions when emotions are involved.

Executive coach Amy Steindler shares the story of one of her clients, a financial advisor, who had a tendency to view things only from his own perspective. Amy worked with him to improve his reality testing skills. She recalls how one of their conversations went:

> CLIENT: I got on a call today with an elderly man to talk about a new investment strategy. I sent all the materials 10 days ahead of the call, and his son inserted himself into the call and said, "We don't have enough information." And we sent him every bit of the information he needed 10 days ago! He just wanted to admonish me in front of his father. He was trying to make me look bad.
>
> COACH: So his goal was to make you look bad?
>
> CLIENT: Yeah, he wanted to prove he was the boss by making me look bad.
>
> COACH: And how did you show up when you were thinking, "He's trying to make me look bad"?
>
> CLIENT: I was tense and defensive. I was showing up for an altercation, and I stopped listening.
>
> COACH: And how would you have shown up if you weren't thinking that thought, "He's trying to make me look bad"? If you assumed his intent was positive?
>
> CLIENT: I would have been calm, asked him what else he needed, and provided it without getting pissed off for the rest of the day. I would have heard him say, "We don't have enough information," instead of "You didn't send us enough information, you idiot," which is the story I made up about it.

This mindset change allowed the client to start questioning his own assumptions and stop thinking about his beliefs as facts. He replaced defensiveness with curiosity. His problem-solving and impulse control also improved. In future meetings, he showed up more relaxed and curious, and he listened to understand, which put him in a better position to help the elderly man and his son.

In his influential book *The Four Agreements* (discussed in chapter 2), don Miguel Ruiz explains that one of the most important agreements to make with ourselves is not to make assumptions. He argues that human beings have a tendency to make assumptions about everything, and the result is we misunderstand situations, take things personally, and end up creating a lot of unhappiness for nothing. "All the sadness and drama you have lived in your life was rooted in making assumptions and taking things personally," he explains.

The reason we make those assumptions is because we don't have the courage to ask for clarification. The solution, then, is to ask questions in a clear way, and to keep on asking until we know what we need to know. And even then, we should remain humble and not assume that we know everything. In this process, courage is key. Courage is not the absence of fear and discomfort; rather, it is taking action and asking the questions *despite* the fear and discomfort.

Reality testing allows us to paint a comprehensive picture of every situation and to challenge our own assumptions and beliefs. It also helps us discern and deal with instances where others have not lived up to our trust. In the next chapter, we will discuss how to apply the last aspect of the positive intent mindset: forgiveness.

— 10 —

Forgiveness

IN THE previous chapters, we discovered the power of realistic optimism, empathy, humility, and reality testing to help us assume positive intention in people who have done something questionable or might have wronged us. But what about situations where we know for sure that the other person has wronged us, repeatedly and intentionally? Does assuming positive intent still apply? The answer is a bit complicated, because we need to relearn what forgiveness means.

Most of us don't know how to properly forgive because we take things too personally. We continue to blame the person who hurt us for how bad we feel long after they have stopped. And we create elaborate grievance stories in which we are the innocent victim and the other person is the guilty villain, and we stay stuck in these stories for a long time.

Ashley, a leader I recently worked with, told me about a previous boss of hers who was very abusive. She recalled in great detail every single time he yelled at her in a meeting. How he would send her work requests late in the evening and expect them to be done by the following morning. How he ignored her requests for breaks and paid time off. As she talked about him, I could feel her getting angrier and angrier as she relived the pain he had inflicted on her.

I finally asked her how long it had been since she worked for that boss. She said it was 18 years ago. I was shocked. I asked her how often she thinks about him. She said it was almost on a weekly basis. Then I asked her whether she believes he still thinks about her that often. She painfully admitted, "I don't think he thought about me at the time when I was working for him. No, he definitely doesn't think about me now." She was continuing to resent him and his actions, without realizing that she was only hurting herself. I remembered the quote often attributed to Nelson Mandela: "Resentment is like drinking poison and then hoping it will kill your enemies."

I asked Ashley to do a mental exercise: If we assume her boss had an average career length, 35 years, how many people would have worked for him in total? We did the math and estimated it would probably be more than 200 people. She was one of at least 200 people that had potentially been abused by this person. He was an equal opportunity offender. She was hardly unique or special.

We then tried to understand what really made her upset now about her old boss. She said, "I am a leader now and I know that he shouldn't have acted that way. Leaders should take care of their people. He should have been kinder." We noticed together how many times she said the world *should*. I helped her understand that whenever she used that word, she was referring to the rules that she has created over time. While very valid, these rules are often unenforceable. And that is why they were still causing her pain.

Slowly, Ashley started to realize that she had taken her old boss's abuse very personally. And that she had allowed him way too much rent-free space in her head for a long time. I finally asked her what it would take for her to forgive him. She replied angrily, "But I don't want to reconcile with him! I don't want him to ever think that what he did was okay."

And that is where she was thinking about forgiveness the wrong way. Forgiveness is not about reconciling with the other person or about making them feel good about themselves. In fact, it has nothing to do with them. I explained to her that forgiveness was only about *her*—finding the peace and not allowing what happened to her 18 years earlier to ruin her present and future. It is not about denying that what happened was painful; it's about not suffering through it over and over. As with so many aspects of the positive intent mindset, pain is inevitable, but suffering is optional.

Gradually, Ashley realized she needed to forgive her old boss—not for him, but for her own peace of mind and sanity. Together we worked through the principles of real forgiveness as discussed by Dr. Fred Luskin in his remarkable book *Forgive for Good*. Luskin defines forgiveness as "the experience of peace and understanding that can be felt in the present moment." He encourages us to forgive by challenging the rigid rules we have for other people's behavior. He stresses that forgiveness does not mean forgetting or denying that painful things have occurred. Rather, forgiveness is the "powerful assertion that bad things will not ruin your today even though they may have spoiled your past."

DR. LUSKIN explains that when we create long-lasting hurt, like Ashley did, it is usually through three main acts:

1. The exaggerated taking of personal offense
2. The blaming of the offender for how we feel
3. The creation of a grievance story

To be able to forgive, we have to push back against each one of those.

First, to reduce our exaggerated taking of *personal offense*, we have to realize how common painful experiences are. Nothing that happens to us, no matter how painful, is unique. Bad bosses are very common. And so are toxic organizational cultures. And insensitive spouses. And car burglaries. And loud people on airplanes. When we intentionally remind ourselves of how statistically common these experiences are, we can start to take them less personally.

Additionally, in most situations the other person does not mean to hurt us personally. It is just the way they act with everyone. Ashley's boss didn't plot out how he was going to make her life miserable every day; that was just his normal behavior. It may have been due to low self-awareness, insecurity, narcissism, or some other internal reason, but it had nothing to do with her. To assume positive intentions in this situation, we only need to assume that people didn't mean to hurt us. It just happened.

The second idea we have to push against is that of *blaming the offender* for how we feel. If we have any chance of moving on, we have to stop associating our distress exclusively with the person who hurt us. When we do that, we take away their power to control our emotions. Their actions have created pain and hurt in the past, but they don't need to continue to. We are responsible for our feelings in the long term and can reduce our suffering.

The final idea that has to be overcome to properly forgive is the *grievance story*. Grievance stories describe the pain and suffering we have endured over time but have not healed from. When we tell these stories, they make us feel hurt or mad all over again. Our chest tightens, our breathing becomes shallow, and our heart rate increases. Not only do these stories hurt us, they actually imprison us for good. They keep us in the past and remind us over and over that we are a victim and will remain a victim. The only way we can forgive and heal is by changing our grievance story.

"Grievances are formed when people are unable to deal successfully with not getting what they wanted," Luskin explains. This is related to the idea of trying to enforce unenforceable rules. He shares the hypothetical example of a hardworking police officer enforcing a 65 mph speed limit on a busy highway stretch. As soon as he turns his radar on, a car whizzes by at 80 mph. The officer tries to start his own vehicle to follow the offending car, but the engine is dead and he is stuck. Then another car speeds by, and another, but the officer's car still won't start. He starts writing tickets for each one of the speeding cars, but he faces a serious problem: He can't issue them to the drivers. Two hours later, his engine still dead, he has written more than 50 unenforceable tickets.

Luskin likens the police officer to each one of us every time someone breaks a rule that we believe in. Every time someone wrongs us and we can't do anything about it, we write them a mental ticket. And just like the speeding tickets clutter the officer's car, our mental tickets clutter our minds. They cause us suffering and feed our grievance stories. "When you try to enforce something over which you have no control, you create a problem for yourself," Luskin explains.

Not all rules are unenforceable. You tell your kids that they shouldn't throw their food on the floor. If they do it anyway, you enforce the rule and put them in time-out. You tell your direct reports not to gossip. If they continue to, you give them a warning.

The problem begins when we think that all the rules are enforceable. Personally, most of my unenforceable rules relate to loud noise: People sitting next to each other on a plane should not talk loudly. People sitting in a coffee shop should not have their phones at maximum volume when they watch videos. Kids sitting on a bus should not play with empty plastic water bottles, making a very annoying noise.

At work I have another set of unenforceable rules: Professionals should return email within 24 hours, colleagues should not hit Reply All in email messages, and universities should not start construction projects at the beginning of the academic year. These rules may sound trivial, but the more of them I have, the more mental tickets I am busy issuing to people I perceive as rude and disrespectful, and the less I enjoy my life.

Forgiveness starts by fighting these self-defeating reactions. We can learn to focus on the impersonal aspect of the hurt, take responsibility for how we feel when someone hurts us, and get rid of our unenforceable rules—transforming our grievance story into a forgiveness story.

THE SCIENTIFIC research shows that how we react to people hurting us impacts not only our mental health but our physical health as well. In one study, research participants were asked to think about hurtful memories they had of real-life offenders. Their immediate emotional and physiological effects were measured using electromyogram (EMG), skin conductance, heart rate, and blood pressure. When the participants thought unforgiving thoughts and nursed grudges against the offenders, negative emotions were prompted, resulting in significant adverse physiological changes. Negative effects on their EMG, skin conductance, and heart rate persisted long after they stopped the unforgiving thoughts.

However, when the participants were asked to cultivate a more empathic perspective and imagined forgiving their offenders, researchers observed greater self-control and fewer significant physiological stress responses. They concluded that a consistently unforgiving mentality may erode health in the long run, whereas forgiveness may actually enhance it. This is especially alarming given that other research has shown that at any point in time, about 69 percent of adults have a lingering gripe of some sort, such as not getting a desired job, being rejected romantically, or having a bad customer service experience.

My friend Sami told me about her dad, who owned a grocery store in Texas. He had built the business from scratch and was very proud of it. Unfortunately, Sami's dad got really sick and needed a liver transplant to save his life. Since Sami lived out of the country and her brother was in medical residency, the family asked a nephew with experience in business to step in and take over the store while the dad was recovering. They were relieved when the nephew accepted the responsibility.

After undergoing the transplant and a lengthy recovery, Sami's dad was ready to go back to work. However, he quickly realized that the nephew had taken advantage of the situation and legally taken over the business, leaving him with nothing.

The family was shocked and furious. They couldn't believe that the nephew would do this, especially at a time when they were so vulnerable. So they decided to sue him.

In the next few weeks, the family would spend every occasion rehashing the story of how the nephew betrayed their trust and stole the business. Every day they would recount the events and suffer. Then one day Sami came home and announced to her family, "I am done suffering from this issue." She decided to humanize her cousin and think of possible reasons why he acted the way he did. Reluctantly, the family joined her and took turns guessing it might have been because of his upbringing, the poverty he faced when he was a young adult, or his many insecurities. Suddenly, they all felt better. And they stopped suffering. "We didn't do this for him, or to save the relationship," Sami explained. "The relationship was not recoverable, and we are still suing him. We did this for ourselves, because we wanted to move on with our lives."

In *The Art of Worldly Wisdom*, a self-help book written in the 15th century, the Spanish philosopher Baltasar Gracián advised, "Don't berate others. There are people with savage tempers who make everything a crime, not out of passion but because of their very character. They condemn everyone, some for what they've done, others for what they will do... They criticize others so exaggeratedly that they make motes into beams in order to poke out eyes. Good-natured people are able to pardon anything. They insist that others had good intentions or went wrong inadvertently." But even if others had bad intentions and meant to hurt us, we can still forgive them. Not because we want *them* to feel better, but because *we* want to feel better.

SO FAR in this chapter, we have discussed forgiveness after someone does something significantly hurtful to us. Can positive intention help us forgive others *before* they have done anything yet? This may sound like an idealistic question, especially in our current society. We live in a world where we don't allow others even a minor slipup. We are all ready to jump in, knives sharpened, to cancel them right away. And of course, many racist, sexist, and otherwise hurtful people who repeatedly and intentionally express offensive views more than deserve to be canceled.

But what about our well-intentioned colleague who misspeaks in a meeting? What about our good-hearted friend who cluelessly reposts an offensive message? What if we assume positive intention until they absolutely prove us wrong? What if we "pre-forgive" them?

This doesn't have to apply only to offensive words and actions. Can we pre-forgive others in our lives by reminding ourselves of who they are and what they have done in the past? My good friend Dr. Eric Marsh shared a question that he always asks himself after someone makes a mistake: "What is this person's track record?" He tries to remind himself of how they behaved towards him in the past and whether this is the first time they have acted this way. Imagine how much forgiveness and grace we can bring to them with this approach. And maybe, next time we mess up, they might treat us with the same grace and pre-forgive us.

This idea is somewhat related to the concept of the emotional bank account popularized by Stephen R. Covey in his best-selling book *The 7 Habits of Highly Successful People*. In every relationship, people make deposits and withdrawals in a joint emotional bank account. When you treat someone well, you add to the balance. When you treat them badly, you make a withdrawal. And the same applies with them. Eric's suggestion is to check the balance before judging the other person harshly and jumping to conclusions. We need to take some time and think, "This is unlike them. I am sure they have a reason. And even if they don't, I choose to forgive them because I trust them."

Another colleague of mine told me about a woman he mentored for a long time. They worked on joint projects, and he always made time to support her and give her advice. Over the years, they became friends outside of work and their families would see each other on weekends. His mentee had a lot of success in her work and became a superstar in her field. He was so proud of her. Then she took on a new job and moved away, and surprisingly, she stopped answering his calls and messages. No matter how hard he tried to connect with her, she didn't respond. She ghosted him.

When he shared the story with me, he explained that he was very hurt. He also admitted, "If she calls me today, I would be happy to hear from her. Because of our history, I'd be willing to forgive her." Despite all the withdrawals she had made in the last two years, there was still enough balance left in the goodwill bank account.

The positive intent mindset requires us to be realistically optimistic about people and their intentions. It calls for empathizing with them and humanizing them. It urges us to be humble, to question our views and remain open-minded to all possibilities. It invites us to test our reality by checking our assumptions, both by ourselves and by talking with others. And it encourages us to forgive people for our own well-being. Now that you have learned the principles of the positive intent mindset, you are ready to start applying them—in your personal life and at work.

— 11 —

The Positive Intent Organization

AT AXIOS, a news website company, assuming positive intention is a core workplace principle. Jim VandeHei, one of the company's founders, explains that when someone appears to do something wrong at Axios, the first priority is to avoid making negative assumptions about them.

How do we build organizations like Axios? VandeHei advises that the key is to ask: "Most of life's problems can be solved instantly if you calmly and clearly ask someone who offended or irritated you what they intended to do or say." He recommends that we make sure we don't ask in a condescending or aggressive way and that we listen to understand. He admits that "yes, some people actually are rotten, or dishonest, or truly out to get you. You shouldn't ignore patterns of toxic behavior. But most people are simply stressed, or clumsy with their words, or innocently screwing up."

In organizations like Axios, leaders are intentional about building cultures centered on accountable positivity.

They give the benefit of the doubt, yet they don't let others get away with bad behaviors. One of the foundations of these types of cultures, as briefly mentioned in chapter 3, is that they adopt a growth mindset about relations. They believe that conflict is normal and healthy and that work relationships have their ups and downs, just like personal ones. So, when a misunderstanding happens, people reach out to each other to clarify intentions. And when serious conflict occurs, they don't give up on the relationship—they seek to repair it with understanding and empathy.

An interesting dynamic exists between leaders and team members in positive intent organizations. Leaders always start with the assumption that team members are intrinsically honest and trustworthy. They believe that everyone cares about their work and wants to do a good job. They think of employees as adults who are willing to take responsibility for their actions and are capable of creating their own schedules and structures without micromanagement. When leaders treat team members this way and tell them that they trust them, most will act accordingly. Positivity begets positivity. Team members will think that leaders are sensitive to their personal issues and interests. They'll see them as fair, reasonable, and interested in members' inputs and opinions on decisions. As we mentioned before, a Cycle of Trust is created based on positive assumptions on both sides.

In this book, we have explored many core behaviors that are helpful in building positive intention organizations. Here is a recap:

- Think about others' mistakes as short-term, specific, and impersonal.
- Dispute your own beliefs by looking for evidence, checking for alternatives, examining possible implications, and questioning the usefulness of the beliefs.
- Humanize others and think of them as people with valid fears and concerns.
- Ask yourself, "Why would a reasonable, decent person act this way?"
- Ask yourself, "What if the other person is trying their best?"
- Ask yourself, "Have I ever done something similar to what the other person did?"
- Replace blind certainty with curiosity about other people.
- Ask open-ended questions that can help reframe situations.
- Overcome confirmation bias by disputing your own assumptions.
- Check your assumptions by talking with others who are close to the situation, and talk with the person in question.
- Do these checks before climbing up the ladder of inference.
- Ask clear questions and listen to understand, not to reply.

- Don't take things personally.
- Don't blame the other person for how you feel.
- Don't create a grievance story.
- Beware of trying to enforce unenforceable rules.
- Consider the other person's track record before judging them harshly.

The secret of these organizations is that their leaders are able to apply these positive intent principles while balancing them with accountability. They give the benefit of the doubt to a team member that has messed up and check with them about what actually happened. They don't sweep insensitive comments or negative behaviors under the rug. They don't shy away from having the necessary and difficult conversations. They share the facts, explain how things look from their perspective, and invite the other person to share theirs. And if the negative behavior is repeated, they have the courage to follow up with consequences.

The positive intent mindset is simple but not easy. It requires us to rewire our brain and fight against our human inclinations and biases. And it is totally worth it. It sets us up to build better relationships, improve trust and collaboration, and enhance our well-being and happiness. Our organizations will benefit, our colleagues will profit, and our lives will be much better. As the great leadership guru Michael Scott said, it is a "win-win-win."

Acknowledgments

I AM DEEPLY GRATEFUL TO many people for their tremendous help and wise advice.

My amazing team at Page Two, Trena White, Jesse Finkelstein, James Harbeck, Carmen Ho, Peter Cocking, and David Marsh, were insightful and supportive. This is my second time working with Page Two, and it's been a great experience.

Several leaders were very gracious and agreed to be interviewed in person, by phone, or by email and share their expertise and time, and others shared valuable ideas in conversations. I owe gratitude to Dr. Lana Bamiro, Dr. Vanessa Beasley, Babs Cheung, Hunter Gatewood, Billy Handmaker, Dave Jeppesen, Tim Johnsen, Dr. Deneese Jones, Kasey Harrington, Tom Henschel, Dr. Sung Lee, Lizna Makhani, Dr. Eric Marsh, Dr. Satish Nadig, Tyler Peavy, Michael Port, Dr. Sam Prater, Henna Pryor, Dr. Kyle Rickner, Dr. Keshma Saujani, Gurpaul Singh, Simran Singh, and Jim Trounson.

My amazing graduate research assistants Maggie Warbritton and Natalie St. John provided vital research support and were always responsive to my requests. My colleagues Marisela Keppes, Erika Seewald, Dr. Ahreum Han, Dr. Patrick Shay, Dr. Ed Schumacher, Dr. Todd Thames, and Dr. Victoria Tian Qin at the Department of Health Care Administration at Trinity University were very supportive and understanding of the time demands that this project required.

Finally, I am always grateful to the countless blessings of the Almighty God for the accomplishment of this and anything else in my life.

Notes

Chapter 1: Our Choice

7   *Epictetus asserted, "It is not":* Epictetus, *The Enchiridion* (Bobbs-Merrill, 1955).

7   *Shakespeare famously wrote:* W. Shakespeare, *Hamlet* (Oxford University Press, 2008).

7   *And John Milton said:* J. Milton, *Paradise Lost* (Oxford University Press, 2008).

10   *Loretta Ross refers to:* L. J. Ross, *Calling In: How to Start Making Change with Those You'd Rather Cancel* (Simon & Schuster, 2025).

12   *The minute we stop:* J. Nguyen, *Don't Believe Everything You Think: Why Your Thinking Is the Beginning & End of Suffering* (One Satori, 2022).

14   *"Whatever anybody says or does":* I. Nooyi, quoted in K. Sola, "20 Business Magnates Share the Wisdom They Learned from Their Fathers," *Forbes*, June 16, 2016, https://www.forbes.com/sites/katiesola/2016/06/16/20-business-magnates-share-the-wisdom-they-learned-from-their-fathers/.

Chapter 2: Why All the Negativity?

20   *Since the development of agriculture:* S. Pinker, *The Better Angels of Our Nature: Why Violence Has Declined* (Penguin Books, 2012).

20 *violence and property crime:* J. Gramlich, "What the Data Says About Crime in the U.S.," Pew Research Center, April 24, 2024, https://www.pewresearch.org/short-reads/2024/04/24/what-the-data-says-about-crime-in-the-us/.

21 *negative words in news headlines:* C. E. Robertson, N. Pröllochs, K. Schwarzenegger et al., "Negativity Drives Online News Consumption," *Nature Human Behaviour* 7 (2023): 812–22, https://doi.org/10.1038/s41562-023-01538-4.

22 *tuning out the negativity:* N. Newman, "Overview and Key Findings of the 2023 Digital News Report," Reuters Institute, June 14, 2023, https://reutersinstitute.politics.ox.ac.uk/digital-news-report/2023/dnr-executive-summary.

23 *"Because we are afraid to ask":* d. M. Ruiz, *The Four Agreements: A Practical Guide to Personal Freedom* (Amber-Allen Publishing, 1997).

24 *called the fundamental attribution error:* P. Healy, "The Fundamental Attribution Error: What It Is & How to Avoid It," Harvard Business School, June 8, 2017, https://online.hbs.edu/blog/post/the-fundamental-attribution-error; S. McLeod, "Fundamental Attribution Error in Psychology," *Simply Psychology*, June 15, 2023, https://www.simplypsychology.org/fundamental-attribution.html.

24 *The interaction between:* L. Ross and R. E. Nisbett, *The Person and the Situation: Perspectives of Social Psychology* (Pinter & Martin Publishers, 2011).

25 *which students would stop:* J. M. Darley and C. D. Batson, "From Jerusalem to Jericho: A Study of Situational and Dispositional Variables in Helping Behavior," *Journal of Personality and Social Psychology* 27, no. 1 (1973): 100–108, https://doi.org/10.1037/h0034449.

25 *participants read a scenario:* H. R. Riggio and A. L. Garcia, "The Power of Situations: Jonestown and the Fundamental Attribution Error," *Teaching of Psychology* 36, no. 2 (2009): 108–12, https://doi.org/10.1080/00986280902739636.

26 *the DMN is where our egos reside:* R. Hougaard and J. Carter, *Compassionate Leadership: How to Do Hard Things in a Human Way* (Harvard Business Review Press, 2022).

27 *we regularly cut ourselves some slack:* Healy, "The Fundamental Attribution Error."

Chapter 3: How Accountable Positivity Works

31 *employee retention and engagement are improved:* R. Cross, T. Opie, G. Pryor, and K. Rollag, "Connect and Adapt: How Network Development and Transformation Improve Retention and Engagement in Employees' First Five Years," *Organizational Dynamics* 47, no. 2 (2018): 115–23, https://doi.org/10.1016/j.orgdyn.2017.08.003.

31 *innovation is sparked:* M. Arena, R. Cross, J. Sims, and M. Uhl-Bien, "How to Catalyze Innovation in Your Organization," *MIT Sloan Management Review* (summer 2017), June 13, 2017, https://sloanreview.mit.edu/article/how-to-catalyze-innovation-in-your-organization/.

31 *productivity is increased:* R. L. Cross, R. D. Martin, and L. M. Weiss, "Mapping the Value of Employee Collaboration," *McKinsey Quarterly*, August 1, 2006, https://www.mckinsey.com/capabilities/people-and-organizational-performance/our-insights/mapping-the-value-of-employee-collaboration.

31 *burnout is reduced:* R. Cross, S. Taylor, and D. Zehner, "Collaboration Without Burnout: Ways to Stay Helpful While Avoiding Overload," *Harvard Business Review*, July–August 2018, https://hbr.org/2018/07/collaboration-without-burnout.

31 *employee well-being:* J. F. Helliwell and R. D. Putnam, "The Social Context of Well-Being," *Philosophical Transactions of the Royal Society of London, Series B, Biological Sciences* 359, no. 1449 (2004): 1435–46, https://doi.org/10.1098/rstb.2004.1522.

31 *career success:* R. Cross, "To Be Happier at Work, Invest More in Your Relationships," *Harvard Business Review*, July 30, 2019, https://hbr.org/2019/07/to-be-happier-at-work-invest-more-in-your-relationships.

31	*This means starting:* "Leadership Effectiveness: Cycle of Trust—Assume Positive Intent," Executive Coaching Network (2016), https://www.executivecoaching.com/wp-content/tips/Leadership_Effectiveness_Cycle_of_Trust_Assume_Positive_Intent.pdf.
32	*let's do a thought experiment:* L. Davey, "Counter-Intuitive Advice on Building Trust," Liane Davey website (2015), https://lianedavey.com/building-trust.
32	*they are more likely to respond:* Davey, "Counter-Intuitive Advice on Building Trust."
32	*It creates reciprocity:* S. R. Covey, *The Speed of Trust: The One Thing That Changes Everything* (Simon & Schuster, 2008).
33	*They adopt a "growth mindset":* R. Friedman, "How High-Performing Teams Build Trust: A Survey of 1,000 Workers Identified Five Behaviors," *Harvard Business Review*, January 10, 2024, https://hbr.org/2024/01/how-high-performing-teams-build-trust; K. D. Ryan and D. K. Oestreich, *Driving Fear Out of the Workplace* (Jossey-Bass, 1998).
35	*leaders see these self-protective:* Ryan and Oestreich, *Driving Fear Out of the Workplace*.
37	*Tom told me he has experienced:* T. Henschel, interview with author, 2023.
40	*The culture at Homeroom:* E. Wade, *The Mac & Cheese Millionaire: Building a Better Business by Thinking Outside the Box* (Wiley, 2024).

Chapter 4: The Limits

45	*"But often telling yourself":* J. R. Detert, "The Problem with Saying 'It's No Big Deal,'" *Harvard Business Review*, August 2021, https://hbr.org/2021/08/the-problem-with-saying-its-no-big-deal.
45	*Their life experiences of being marginalized:* Dr. D. Jones, interview with author, 2024.
46	*Ruth was not happy with the advice:* R. Terry, "The Problem with Assuming Positive Intent," Medium, February 26, 2020, https://forge.medium.com/the-problem-with-assuming-positive-intent-ea8385ce961d.

47	*Lena Tenney, the coordinator of public engagement:* Terry, "The Problem with Assuming Positive Intent."
48	*they perceive it as ignoring the impact:* "Does anyone else think 'assume positive intent' is so toxic??" Reddit, https://www.reddit.com/r/work/comments/100tk1g/does_anyone_else_think_assume_positive_intent_is/; "Assuming Best Intentions is Bullsh*t," MetaFilter, December 10, 2019, https://ask.metafilter.com/340110/Assuming-Best-Intentions-is-Bullsht; "The Benefit of Doubt," Competitiveness Mindset Institute, October 16, 2021, https://www.competitivenessmindset.org/post/the-benefit-of-doubt; M. Treanor, "The Pitfalls of 'Assuming Good Intentions': Why Behavior Matters More in Leadership," LinkedIn, March 6, 2023, https://www.linkedin.com/pulse/pitfalls-assuming-good-intentions-why-behaviour-more-mags/; A. H. Salopek and M. S. Eastin, "Toxic Positivity Intentions: An Image Management Approach to Upward Social Comparison and False Self-Presentation," *Journal of Computer-Mediated Communication* 29, no. 3 (2024), https://doi.org/10.1093/jcmc/zmae003; A. B. Yang, "What's Wrong with 'Assume Positive Intent'? Sometimes Intentions Are Not Positive," *Work Better* June 22, 2023, https://www.workbetter.media/p/whats-wrong-with-assume-positive; N. Lane, "Stop Using 'Assume Positive Intent' in Your Team Agreements," LinkedIn, January 13, 2023, https://www.linkedin.com/pulse/stop-using-assume-positive-intent-your-team-nevada-lane-msod/; B. Careau, "You're Assuming Positive Intent. Are You Owning Your Impact?" LinkedIn, November 17, 2022, https://www.linkedin.com/pulse/youre-assuming-positive-intent-you-owning-your-impact-bibi-careau-/; "Balancing Optimism with Toxic Positivity: When Looking on the Bright Side Becomes Too Much," *Lead Read Today*, The Ohio State University Fischer College of Business, August 6, 2024, https://fisher.osu.edu/blogs/leadreadtoday/balancing-optimism-toxic-positivity-when-looking-bright-side-becomes-too-much.

49	*With people we know:* S. R. Covey, *The Speed of Trust: The One Thing That Changes Everything* (Simon & Schuster, 2008).
50	*The evidence is in fact overwhelming:* R. Bregman, *Humankind: A Hopeful History* (Bloomsbury, 2019).
51	*Bregman offers a practical argument for assuming positive intentions:* Bregman, *Humankind*.
51	*better at detecting lies:* N. L. Carter and J. M. Weber, "Not Pollyannas: Higher Generalized Trust Predicts Lie Detection Ability," *Social Psychological and Personality Science* 1, no. 3 (2010): 274–79, https://doi.org/10.1177/1948550609360261.
51	*expert on fraudsters, psychologist Maria Konnikova:* M. Konnikova, *The Confidence Game: The Psychology of the Con and Why We Fall for It Every Time* (Viking, 2016).
51	*"That's a small price to pay":* Bregman, *Humankind*.

Chapter 5: Making It Work

53	*In his excellent book:* S. O'Neil, *Be Where Your Feet Are: Seven Principles to Keep You Present, Grounded, and Thriving* (St. Martin's Essentials, 2021).
55	*Researchers David Yeager, Kyle Dobson, and Andrea Dittman:* D. Yeager, K. Dobson, and A. Dittmann, "A Transparency Statement Transforms Community-Police Interactions," preprint, Research Square (2022), https://doi.org/10.21203/rs.3.rs-1726104/v1.
56	*Transparency statements are now being:* D. Yeager, *10 to 25: The Science of Motivating Young People* (Avid Reader Press/Simon & Schuster, 2024).
57	*And almost instantly:* Dr. K. Rickner, interview with author, 2024.
57	*Author and activist Simran:* S. J. Singh, *The Light We Give: How Sikh Wisdom Can Transform Your Life* (Riverhead Books, 2022).
57	*In one interview, he related:* Rachel Martin, "Letting Go of Hate by Questioning the Very Idea of Evil," *All Things Considered*, NPR, May 21, 2023,

https://www.npr.org/2023/05/21/1176864308/religion-hate-evil-spirituality-simran-jeet-singh-sikh.

61 *trust is very individual:* C. A. M. Sutherland, N. S. Burton, J. B. Wilmer, G. A. M. Blokland, L. Germine, R. Palermo, J. R. Collova, and G. Rhodes, "Individual Differences in Trust Evaluations Are Shaped Mostly by Environments, Not Genes," *Proceedings of the National Academy of Sciences of the United States of America* 117, no. 19 (2020): 10218–24, https://doi.org/10.1073/pnas.1920131117.

62 *Our decision whether to trust:* F. Marini, C. A. M. Sutherland, B. Ostrovska, and M. Manassi, "Three's a Crowd: Fast Ensemble Perception of First Impressions of Trustworthiness," *Cognition* 239 (2023): 105540, https://doi.org/10.1016/j.cognition.2023.105540.

62 *In* Talking to Strangers, *Malcolm Gladwell:* M. Gladwell, *Talking to Strangers* (Little, Brown and Company, 2019).

62 *Further complications arise when:* W. Ickes, "Empathic Accuracy: Its Links to Clinical, Cognitive, Developmental, Social, and Physiological Psychology," in *The Social Neuroscience of Empathy*, eds. J. Decety and W. Ickes (Oxford University Press, 2009), 57–70, https://doi.org/10.7551/mitpress/9780262012973.003.0006.

63 *number of remote workers:* G. Carpenter, "How Many People Work Remotely?," B2B Reviews, December 2, 2024, https://www.b2breviews.com/remote-work-statistics/.

63 *notes the journalist and workplace expert:* R. Knight, "How to Improve Your Soft Skills as a Remote Worker," *Harvard Business Review*, January 8, 2024, https://hbr.org/2024/01/how-to-improve-your-soft-skills-as-a-remote-worker.

64 *shared reality is cultivated where people:* Knight, "How to Improve Your Soft Skills as a Remote Worker."

Chapter 6: Realistic Optimism

65 *according to Martin Seligman:* M. E. P. Seligman, *Learned Optimism: How to Change Your Mind and Your Life* (Vintage, 2006).

66 *Optimistic patients tend to know:* N. M. Radcliffe and W. M. P. Klein, "Dispositional, Unrealistic, and Comparative Optimism: Differential Relations with the Knowledge and Processing of Risk Information and Beliefs About Personal Risk," *Personality and Social Psychology Bulletin* 28, no. 6 (2002): 836–46, https://doi.org/10.1177/0146167202289012; L. S. Solberg Nes and S. C. Segerstrom, "Dispositional Optimism and Coping: A Meta-Analytic Review," *Personality and Social Psychology Review* 10, no. 3 (2006): 235–51, https://doi.org/10.1207/s15327957pspr1003_3.

66 *less likely to develop chronic conditions:* S. A. Everson, G. A. Kaplan, D. E. Goldberg, and J. T. Salonen, "Hypertension Incidence Is Predicted by High Levels of Hopelessness in Finnish Men," *Hypertension* 35, no. 2 (2000): 561–67, https://doi.org/10.1161/01.hyp.35.2.561; L. D. Kubzansky, D. Sparrow, P. Vokonas, and I. Kawachi, "Is the Glass Half Empty or Half Full? A Prospective Study of Optimism and Coronary Heart Disease in the Normative Aging Study," *Psychosomatic Medicine* 63, no. 6 (2001): 910–16, https://doi.org/10.1097/00006842-200111000-00009; L. Brydon, C. Walker, A. J. Wawrzyniak, H. Chart, and A. Steptoe, "Dispositional Optimism and Stress-Induced Changes in Immunity and Negative Mood," *Brain, Behavior, and Immunity* 23, no. 6 (2009): 810–16, https://doi.org/10.1016/j.bbi.2009.02.018; M. F. Scheier, K. A. Matthews, J. F. Owens, R. Schulz, M. W. Bridges, G. J. Magovern, and C. S. Carver, "Optimism and Rehospitalization After Coronary Artery Bypass Graft Surgery," *Archives of Internal Medicine* 159, no. 8 (1999): 829–35, https://doi.org/10.1001/archinte.159.8.829; V. S. Helgeson, "Cognitive Adaptation, Psychological Adjustment, and Disease Progression Among Angioplasty Patients: 4 Years Later," *Health Psychology* 22, no. 1 (2003): 30–38, https://doi.org/10.1037//0278-6133.22.1.30; J. A.

Cauley, S. F. Smagula, K. M. Hovey, J. Wactawski-Wende, C. A. Andrews, C. J. Crandall, and H. A. Tindle, "Optimism, Cynical Hostility, Falls, and Fractures: The Women's Health Initiative Observational Study (WHI-OS)," *Journal of Bone and Mineral Research* 32, no. 2 (2017): 221-29, https://doi.org/10.1002/jbmr.2984.

66 *Cancer patients who are more optimistic:* P. J. Allison, C. Guichard, and L. Gilain, "A Prospective Investigation of Dispositional Optimism as a Predictor of Health-Related Quality of Life in Head and Neck Cancer Patients," *Quality of Life Research* 9, no. 8 (2000): 951-60, https://doi.org/10.1023/a:1008931906253; C. S. Carver, C. Pozo, S. D. Harris, V. Noriega, M. F. Scheier, D. S. Robinson, and K. C. Clark, "How Coping Mediates the Effect of Optimism on Distress: A Study of Women with Early-Stage Breast Cancer," *Journal of Personality and Social Psychology* 65, no. 2 (1999): 375-90, https://doi.org/10.1037//0022-3514.65.2.375.

66 *intrinsic motivation to work:* F. Luthans, "Positive Organizational Behavior (POB): Implications for Leadership and HR Development and Motivation," in *Motivation and Leadership at Work*, eds. R. M. Steers, L. W. Porter, and G. A. Bigley (McGraw-Hill/Irwin, 2003), 178-98.

66 *results in more well-being overall:* D. Strutton and J. Lumpkin, "Relationship Between Optimism and Coping Strategies in the Work Environment," *Psychological Reports* 71, no. 3 (1992): 1179-86, https://doi.org/10.2466/pro.1992.71.3f.1179; P. Norman, S. Collins, M. Conner, R. Martin, and J. Rance, "Attributions, Cognitions, and Coping Styles: Teleworkers' Reactions to Work-Related Problems," *Journal of Applied Social Psychology* 25, no. 2 (1995): 117-28, https://doi.org/10.1111/j.1559-1816.1995.tb01587.x; P. M. Podsakoff and S. B. MacKenzie, "Impact of Organizational Citizenship Behavior on Organizational Performance: A Review and Suggestions

for Future Research," *Human Performance* 10, no. 2 (1997): 133–51, https://doi.org/10.1207/s15327043hup1002_5; J. Chiok Foong Loke, "Leadership Behaviours: Effects on Job Satisfaction, Productivity, and Organizational Commitment," *Journal of Nursing Management* 9, no. 4 (2001): 191–204, https://doi.org/10.1046/j.1365-2834.2001.00231.x; J. K. Harter, F. L. Schmidt, and C. L. Keyes, "Well-Being in the Workplace and Its Relationship to Business Outcomes: A Review of the Gallup Studies," in *Flourishing: The Positive Person and the Good Life*, eds. C. L. Keyes and J. Haidt (American Psychological Association, 2003), 205–24; J. H. Gavin and R. O. Mason, "The Virtuous Organization: The Value of Happiness in the Workplace," *Organizational Dynamics* 33 (2004): 379–92, https://psycnet.apa.org/doi/10.1016/j.orgdyn.2004.09.005.

66 *more productive than pessimists:* M. E. P. Seligman and P. Schulman, "Explanatory Style as a Predictor of Productivity and Quitting Among Life Insurance Agents," *Journal of Personality and Social Psychology* 50 (1986): 832–38.

66 *more career satisfaction:* D. Spurk, S. Kauffeld, L. Barthauer, and N. S. Heinemann, "Fostering Networking Behavior, Career Planning and Optimism, and Subjective Career Success: An Intervention Study," *Journal of Vocational Behavior* 87 (2015): 134–44, https://psycnet.apa.org/doi/10.1016/j.jvb.2014.12.007.

66 *A Harvard Business Review study:* M. Gielan, "The Financial Upside of Being an Optimist," *Harvard Business Review*, March 12, 2019, https://hbr.org/2019/03/the-financial-upside-of-being-an-optimist.

Chapter 7: Empathy

79 *Dave recalls, "We had a lot of interesting":* D. Jeppesen, interview with author, 2024.

81 *brought a group of Manchester United:* M. Levine, A. Prosser, D. Evans, and S. Reicher, "Identity and Emergency Intervention: How Social Group Membership and

83   Inclusiveness of Group Boundaries Shape Helping Behavior," *Personality and Social Psychology Bulletin* 31, no. 4 (2005): 443–53, https://doi.org/10.1177/0146167204271651.
83   *Negative patriotism is about:* A. D. Grant, "I Was Wrong About the Olympics," *Granted*, August 11, 2024, https://adamgrant.substack.com/p/i-was-wrong-about-the-olympics.
85   *Simran was desperate for something:* S. J. Singh, *The Light We Give: How Sikh Wisdom Can Transform Your Life* (Riverhead Books, 2022).
86   *an executive's to-do list:* R. F. Baumeister and J. Tierney, *Willpower: Rediscovering the Greatest Human Strength* (Penguin Books, 2012).
86   *we may choose to start helping:* C. Kininmonth, "Brené Brown Top Tip: Assume Others Are Doing the Best They Can," Growth Faculty, February 24, 2019, https://thegrowthfaculty.com/articles/BrenBrowntoptipassumeothersaredoingthebesttheycan.
87   *stay away from judgment and attempt:* B. Brown, *Dare to Lead: Brave Work. Tough Conversations. Whole Hearts.* (Random House, 2018).
87   *productive than emotional empathy:* J. Zaki, "How to Sustain Your Empathy in Difficult Times," *Harvard Business Review*, January–February 2024, https://hbr.org/2024/01/how-to-sustain-your-empathy-in-difficult-times.
89   *nuclear war that might destroy:* R. F. Kennedy, *Thirteen Days: A Memoir of the Cuban Missile Crisis* (W. W. Norton & Company, 1969); D. Munton and D. A. Welch, *The Cuban Missile Crisis: A Concise History* (Oxford University Press, 2011); M. Dobbs, *One Minute to Midnight: Kennedy, Khrushchev, and Castro on the Brink of Nuclear War* (Knopf, 2008); S. M. Stern, *The Cuban Missile Crisis in American Memory: Myths Versus Reality* (Stanford University Press, 2012); G. T. Allison and P. Zelikow, *Essence of Decision: Explaining the Cuban Missile Crisis* (Pearson, 1999).

89 *The author advised:* B. H. Liddell Hart, *Deterrent or Defense: A Fresh Look at the West's Military Position* (Kessinger Publishing, 2010).

Chapter 8: Humility

93 *The two young fish continue:* D. F. Wallace, "This Is Water," commencement address at Kenyon College (2005).

96 *In her insightful:* Lynn Carnes, "Raging Bitch to Engaging Coach | Lynn Carnes | TEDxTryon," TEDx Talks, October 9, 2015, video, 13:16, https://www.youtube.com/watch?v=9rCbEzx5aSo.

97 *"The test of open-mindedness is":* W. Hare, "Open-Mindedness in Moral Education: Three Contemporary Approaches," *Journal of Moral Education* 16, no. 2 (1987): 99-107, https://doi.org/10.1080/03057240.1987.1075355 7.

97 *means a willingness to subject:* J. S. Spiegel, "Open-Mindedness and Intellectual Humility," *Theory and Research in Education* 10, no. 1 (2012): 27-38, https://doi.org/10.1177/1477878512437472.

97 *"I forbid myself":* B. Franklin, *The Autobiography of Benjamin Franklin* (Arcturus Publishing, 2019), 42.

98 *Franklin aimed to start his sentences:* S. Snow, "A New Way to Become More Open-Minded," *Harvard Business Review*, November 20, 2018, https://hbr.org/2018/11/a-new-way-to-become-more-open-minded.

98 *we can't be curious about someone:* K. Murphy, *You're Not Listening: What You're Missing and Why It Matters* (Celadon Books, 2020).

98 *"the fine art of drawing someone out":* E. H. Schein, *Humble Inquiry: The Gentle Art of Asking Instead of Telling* (Berrett-Koehler Publishers, 2013), 21.

100 *seek information that challenges:* M. Gervais, *The First Rule of Mastery: Stop Worrying About What People Think of You* (Harvard Business Review Press, 2023).

100   *One way to deal with:* Gervais, *The First Rule of Mastery*.
102   *The goal of the assessments:* D. Frye, "The Doctor Learns Humility," *Psychology Today*, December 31, 2022, https://www.psychologytoday.com/us/blog/my-side-of-the-couch/202212/the-doctor-learns-humility; "Why Relationships Matter," *Psychology Today*, https://www.psychologytoday.com/us/basics/relationships.
104   *Epictetus, the stoic:* Epictetus, *The Discourses of Epictetus, with the Encheridion and Fragments*, trans. George Long (Hurst & Co. Publishers, 1890).

Chapter 9: Reality Testing

109   *assumptions unchecked and untested:* P. M. Senge, *The Fifth Discipline Fieldbook: Strategies and Tools for Building a Learning Organization* (Crown Currency, 1994).
114   *author Melody Wilding:* M. Wilding, "How to Stop Taking Work So Personally," *Harvard Business Review*, October 20, 2023, https://hbr.org/2023/10/how-to-stop-taking-work-so-personally.
117   *he showed up more relaxed and curious:* A. Steindler, "The Magic of Reality Testing: How Assuming Positive Intent Changes Everything," Leadership Call, August 3, 2021, https://leadershipcall.com/index.php/2021/08/03/the-magic-of-reality-testing-how-assuming-positive-intent-changes-everything/.
117   *He argues that human beings have:* D. M. Ruiz, *The Four Agreements: A Practical Guide to Personal Freedom* (Tarcher, 1997).

Chapter 10: Forgiveness

120   *attributed to Nelson Mandela:* D. Horsey, "Nelson Mandela Transformed Himself and Then His Nation," *Los Angeles Times*, December 6, 2013, https://www.latimes.com/opinion/topoftheticket/la-na-tt-nelson-mandela-20131206-story.html.

121   *Dr. Fred Luskin in his remarkable book:* F. Luskin, *Forgive for Good: A Proven Prescription for Health and Happiness* (HarperOne, 2003).

126   *consistently unforgiving mentality may erode:* C. van Oyen Witvliet, T. E. Ludwig, and K. L. Vander Laan, "Granting Forgiveness or Harboring Grudges: Implications for Emotion, Physiology, and Health," *Psychological Science* 12, no. 2 (2001): 117–23, https://doi.org/10.1111/1467-9280.00320.

126   *69 percent of adults have a lingering:* B. Robinson, "New Study Shows the Mental and Physical Harm of Holding Workplace Grudges," *Forbes*, February 5, 2022, https://www.forbes.com/sites/bryanrobinson/2022/02/05/new-study-shows-the-mental-and-physical-harm-of-holding-workplace-grudges/.

127   *the Spanish philosopher Baltasar Gracián:* B. Gracián, *The Art of Worldly Wisdom: A Pocket Oracle* (Doubleday, 1992).

128   *Dr. Eric Marsh shared:* Dr. E. Marsh, interview with author, 2023.

128   *emotional bank account popularized by:* S. R. Covey, *The 7 Habits of Highly Effective People: Powerful Lessons in Personal Change* (Free Press, 2004).

Chapter 11: The Positive Intent Organization

131   *VandeHei advises:* J. VandeHei, "Simplest Workplace Principle: Assume Positive Intent," *Axios*, June 4, 2022, https://www.axios.com/2022/06/03/simple-workplace-principle-assume-positive-intent.

132   *And when serious:* R. Friedman, "How High-Performing Teams Build Trust; A Survey of 1,000 Workers Identified Five Behaviors," *Harvard Business Review*, January 10, 2024, https://hbr.org/2024/01/how-high-performing-teams-build-trust; K. D. Ryan and D. K. Oestreich, *Driving Fear Out of the Workplace* (Jossey-Bass, 1998).

132   *a Cycle of Trust:* Ryan and Oestreich, *Driving Fear Out of the Workplace*.

About Amer Kaissi

AMER KAISSI is an award-winning professor of leadership at Trinity University in Texas and the author of five books. He is an executive coach who works with high-performing leaders and teams.

Amer is also a professional speaker, speaking on leadership topics at hundreds of organizations and professional conferences all over the world.

He grew up in Beirut, Lebanon, and is an avid football (soccer) fan. He lives with his wife in San Antonio and has two adult children in college.

Join the Positive Intent Movement!

Invite Amer to speak to your team or organization: akaissi@trinity.edu

Write a review of this book on your favorite online retailer's website or online forum

Connect with Amer on LinkedIn at www.linkedin.com/in/amer-kaissi-ph-d-38258919

Sign up for Amer's newsletter *Leaders Are Readers* at amerkaissi.com